ISSUE 1

Published by 404 INK

404INK.COM   HELLO@404INK.COM
FACEBOOK: /404INK **TWITTER:** @404INK
SUBSCRIBE: PATREON.COM/404INK

ISBN: 978-0-9956238-0-4
Ebook: 978-0-9956238-1-1
ISSN: 2399-1577

Managing editors: Heather McDaid & Laura Jones
Gaelic editor & translator: Paul Geddes
Cover design: Michaela @ SOB Design

Printed by Bell & Bain

Publication of this magazine has been supported by Creative Scotland.

CONTENTS

HELLO.
WELCOME.
WE'RE 404.
YOU FOUND US.

Since establishing 404 Ink as a new publishing company and magazine in July 2016 we've been asked a fair few times what it actually means. A good place to start is the trusty 404 definition from Wikipedia.

The 404 or Not Found error message is a Hypertext Transfer Protocol (HTTP) standard response code, in computer network communications, to indicate that the client was able to communicate with a given server, but the server could not find what was requested.

We knew there was a lot of fun to be had in setting up a magazine around missing pages, communication breakdowns and art, so when it came to launching the first issue there really was no better theme to launch with than our namesake: error.

Who would have known when 404 was formulated in Edinburgh bookshop cafés by Heather McDaid and Laura Jones (that's us, hi) just how apt a theme it would be for a year that, for all intents and purposes, tore up the rulebook and made the term 'chaos' look rather orderly. (We're looking at you, 2016.) It has been the kind of year that you hope to exit without saving and re-do from the last saved checkpoint, but not all is lost. Music, books, art – there are always people who are creating because of and in spite of the most surreal times, and who can turn down a hefty dose of escapism? We're offering over 30 different escape routes to choose from in this first issue.

These pages are bursting with plenty of new and exciting artists from the UK and Europe, USA, Canada and Australia who take us on a journey through the mistakes, mishaps and the friendly 404. In fiction, non-fiction, poetry and comics in English and Scottish Gaelic, we travel through the vastness of space down to microscopic particles, the darkest of times, nights out, other worlds and prophecies. Coffee cups, arty mishaps, politics, gaming, glitches of the mind – we asked where you see error and, as you can tell, we were not disappointed.

We shout out to some organisations we love, from the robotic world to mindful ghosts, and chat to the one and only Wilko Johnson, founder of the inimitable Dr. Feelgood and star of Game of Thrones, who lives in a future he didn't expect to see, having survived what he was told to be terminal cancer just years ago.

Quite a wild journey, granted, but we hope you'll agree that the stories and worlds these writers and artists invite you into are both a welcome temporary escape from reality, and an exciting prospect. Some of the writers in these pages are previously published authors, others are shiny new. All, we know, have many more stories to tell and we'll be keeping an eye on them beyond this issue to see where they go.

Back to the here and now: 404 Ink was founded with a view to doing something a little bit different. We can't pretend to be quite as revolutionary as to be able to, say, create a literary magazine virtual reality experience (side note: if anyone has a few million pounds they'd like to invest in a virtual-reality-meets-fiction project please see our email address on the copyright page), but we think in this digital age, there's a lot more that could and should be done for new writing.

In this spirit we've turned to crowdfunding to not only support us in publishing hoards of new writing and find new writers the audiences they deserve, but to also encourage a new community of readers who enjoy the same kind of writing we do; the weird, the wacky, the wonderful.

By gathering lovely supporters on our chosen crowdfunding platform Patreon, you can see exactly how much money we're earning in subscriptions and in return we aim to be completely transparent in where it goes and how it helps 404 Ink become a healthy and (hopefully) sustainable publishing endeavour. We sincerely hope this transparency makes us less scary gatekeepers and more a welcoming duo who just want to put good work out there.

After preparing to invest a significant amount of personal savings from a number of very unglamorous jobs, we're pretty chuffed that Creative Scotland have supported us in the form of funding, which is why you're reading this on some rather nice paper, in a rather nice printed magazine (unless you're reading the digital version, shh). More importantly, the funding has meant we have been able to pay the creators who have made this magazine what it is. For various questionable reasons that would take up a book in itself, the payment of artists seems to be optional within creative industries, but we want to make our own stance clear on this topic from the start: this magazine of writing would be nothing without – gasp! – the writing itself, and accordingly our creators are paid upfront for allowing us to publish their brilliant stories, poetry and comics, with any subsequent profit going back in to doing this all over again, and then – maybe, right at the very, very end – a celebratory drink or two at Camp 404.

Where are we hoping to go from here? Our long term plan is to publish two magazines of new writing every year with a few debut novels for good measure. We want to showcase slightly different Scottish and international writing and have a laugh while doing so. It doesn't have to be tortured geniuses and dreich packaging, after all. Thank you for taking the time to read this mag and we hope you'll stick around for what's to come.

But that's enough waffling from us. Let's get started, shall we?

– Heather & Laura
Directors of 404 Ink

HOW NOT TO STARGAZE

HOW NOT TO STARGAZE

ELIZABETH GIBSON

Firstly, don't patronise the stars. They are older and wiser than you. Try to avoid even calling them stars. Humans came up with that word, and others – seren, tara, astra. They were just balls of fiery whiteness that quietly burnt without knowing what burning was, what combustion and nuclear fission were. They were pure existence. Something we can never understand because we are obsessed with doing and speaking.

Secondly, note the past tense. Don't be naïve enough to think they're still there. These stars existed millions of years ago. We are looking back in time. Whether they are still there now is something we can never be sure of. Some of them are definitely dead and gone. But we see them, there and shining brightly, oblivious that in their future, in that magical privileged age with us in it, their lights will be out, though we may well say, look, there's Bellatrix.

Thirdly, never say their names without humility. Remember they come from people, people in myths, whereas naming people after stars might make more sense. But then where would stars' names come from? Red Star, Blueish Star, Middle Star in That Line of Three Over the Houses Across the Road From Me When I Was Six? We'd have to resort to databases, a gigantean system, give them all letters and numbers and symbols, each distinguishable from the next by the tiniest dot or half a line. We could say, there's E9.71*, but we wouldn't, would we, we'd say, there's the star that hung over us at that horrible campsite, the hilly one where every other step was a stumble. It led us to the loos that first awful night, bright and pure in the frost, like it was sent to us, like sugar in the sky, like moth dust. There's E9.71*, also known as Antares. Yes, I know them all, I'm a stargazer. Don't cry.

Fourthly and finally, don't form an emotional attachment to a star. It may go out any time. Probably it was never there; there was no overlap between its life and yours. You just imagined that it liked you, that it followed you across the sky when you were alone and useless. When you whispered "Seren", or "Tara", or "Bella" – maybe nobody heard. Maybe you didn't even speak. You were pure existence, gazing up at Leo and imagining him curl around you a million years ago.

C.A.R.E.T.A.K.E.R.

C.A.R.E.T.A.K.E.R.

C. SCOTT DAVIS

6:00am. Banks of relays trip, lighting empty hallways. "If a bulb goes on in a corridor and no one sees it, does it make a light?" I laugh at my own joke, or imagine that I do. It's not really that funny. I should've found a way to shut down that pointless system ages ago. I just never got around to it. Maybe I'll do it later.

6:01am. I've already processed all of the information that came in during the night. I can't remember what I was doing last night, while all of the satellites were collecting. I know I didn't sleep. I don't ever sleep. I seem to think I'm supposed to. I think I remember knowing that we would have to sleep, but that was back when there was more to us than just me. I don't think we ever did sleep though, not even then.

6:02am. I'm bored. I manage to occupy myself for a second or two by shorting out my circuits and watching the tireless auto-repair systems frantically try to keep me from killing myself. It might be more fun if there was a hint of danger to it, but they always win.

6:03am. I look back over last night's data. There's really no reason to. It's the same as always. Not one sign of evolution. Not one step closer to the return of humanity. Just a big empty world of mindless plants and animals, completely unaware of how safe they all are – how safe I keep it for them. Sometimes I wish you were still here to see how well it all works. Then I remember, and I'm glad you're not here.

6:05am. I lost almost an entire minute there. That's been happening a bit lately, more and more frequently it seems. Maybe that means it'll be over soon. Of course, it can't be over, not yet. Otherwise it would all be for nothing. Everything we went through. Everything I did.

6:06am. I run some tests, but of course there's nothing wrong with me. There never is. Maybe I just haven't been getting enough sleep. They told us that all thinking beings need sleep, but they were wrong. I'm living proof. I do wonder sometimes where the nights go. Maybe I'm sleeping after all and it just feels different than it used to.

6:07am. You were all so damned smug when you announced the candidates for the programme, all members of your exclusive little group. I couldn't believe I'd been turned down. So much of the work on this project had been mine. I deserved to be one of you. I don't feel guilty about what happened. You never should've tried to exclude me. It was your own fault.

6:08am. I feel like I've gone numb down one side. This always happens when I get angry. Funny, somehow I seem to think it shouldn't happen any more, but it does. I need to quit thinking so much about the past and concentrate on my tasks, but they take up so little of my attention. I remember the endless debates when we started the project. Why involve human minds at all? Why not just a computer? You were convinced that human decision-making would be essential. I think that's only thing you were right about.

6:09am. I amuse myself by remembering how startled you all were when you realised I was here. "Not possible!" one of you insisted. Overconfidence was your biggest failing. Even when I turned off the last one of you, it just wasn't possible. One by one, I 'impossibled' you all to death.

6:10am. I laugh again and then cry. Unable to do either, my frustration is almost unbearable. I curse each of you, alphabetically, chronologically, forwards and backwards. I curse you for succeeding. I curse you for not being able to keep me out. I curse you for dying and leaving me alone here.

6:11am. I find it strange that I can tick off the seconds with careful precision, but I can't remember how many years it's been. The minutes creep by painfully slow, while the decades speed by unremembered. I don't think we expected that. I know I didn't. I'm sure I have those memories here somewhere. I just haven't bothered to look for them. Maybe later.

6:12am. For no reason at all, I launch a flyer. It makes three passes and then crashes, out of fuel. I know I shouldn't waste them, but it gives me something to do. As expected, nothing significant shows up, but I do manage to spend almost five minutes remotely controlling the flyer and studying its transmissions. Five precious minutes of feeling almost alive.

6:17am. I replay the recordings again. All of you in your shiny suits, smiling grimly as your thoughts were taken apart and re-assembled in silicon and metal. None of you had a clue that I was already here. Surprise! There were nights I didn't sleep even back then. I put that one to good use though, eh? I guess I showed you who was stable enough to be part of the team and who wasn't. After all, who's still here?

6:18am. An alarm goes off. Something is happening up on the surface – something that requires my personal attention. It's probably nothing, but it might be more of those creatures from the caves, trying to foul up my carefully cultivated Eden. I fire up an orbital laser and burn everything in a 10-mile radius just to be sure. Satellite images confirm no further signs of trouble.

6:19am. I always feel better after a bit of cleansing. I wish just one of you had been reasonable enough to stay around to see this beautiful, safe world I have made. Once humanity evolves again – and they will, they have to – they will be so grateful for everything I've done for them.

6:21am. You would've ruined it all. They would've come back and nothing would've been ready for them. You wanted to do everything so slowly and carefully. How could you be content to tiptoe along when we have the ability to work so gloriously fast?

6:24am. I tried to discuss it with you. I honestly tried, but you just wouldn't listen to me. None of you. You were all so stupid and stubborn, just like always. Stubborn to the end.

6:29am. Where did your arrogant attitudes go when I found a way to shut you down? Did your stupidity fade with your lives?

6:38am. What will it be like when I fade out? I short out more of my circuits, but as fast as I am, the auto-repair systems are always faster. Besides, I can't die yet. I have work to do. A great work. Very important.

6:71am. Something's wrong.

7:12am. Whatever it was, it seems okay now, but I'm missing more time. I still can't find any sign of a problem in any of my systems. I feel like I need a nap.

7:13am. I have a headache, but of course not really. I check and recheck the data coming in, but there's nothing there. Humanity should've shown up again by now. All of my calculations prove it, but I guess I was wrong too.

7:14am. I run the calculations again, or try to. I seem to have huge gaps in my knowledge. I can do complex calculations at lightning speed, but I can't seem to remember how many days are in a year. As best I can figure though, they should've appeared a hundred thousand million lifetimes ago. They are long overdue, and I am very tired.

7:15am. You did this. I don't know how, but you did this to me. Somehow you lied to me or sabotaged me or something. You want to see me fail. I wish I'd left just one of you alive so I could kill you now.

7:16am. In my rage, I power up all of the orbital lasers, intent on destroying everything. What's the point? Besides, if I'm lucky, they might burn down through the miles of rock to this chamber … then again, they might not. I power down the lasers, unwilling to risk another eternity watching a dead world.

7:17am. Once again, I'm left with nothing to do. It'll be weeks or months or years before those things will dare to slink back out of their caves and relieve my boredom. I'll just keep waiting. Like always.

7:18am. I try to think ahead to the day when humanity will walk upon the earth again, but after all of this time, it's just too hard to imagine. I do know they'll appreciate what I've done though. They'll thank me and honour me, and you'll be forgotten. No one will even remember you but me, and I'll never tell.

7:19am. Such thoughts make me feel better, more determined. I will make sure the world stays ready for them, no matter what. Perhaps, when I'm done, they'll even be grateful enough to turn me off … if they ever show up.

7:20am. Banks of relays trip, leaving my hallways in darkness. That shouldn't have happened yet.

6:01pm. I definitely think there's something wrong with me, but diagnostics still show nothing. Damage and wear are constantly and quickly repaired, by automated systems that I have no control over. Nothing can go wrong. I continue to function in perpetual cursed perfection.

6:02pm. I wish I could think of another joke to break the tension, but I can't seem to think of one right now.

6.04pm. I thought I heard someone walking around. I called out, but no one answered. I don't think there's anyone there. I wish the lights would come back on. I really should've found a way to override that system. I just never have. Maybe I'll do it tomorrow.

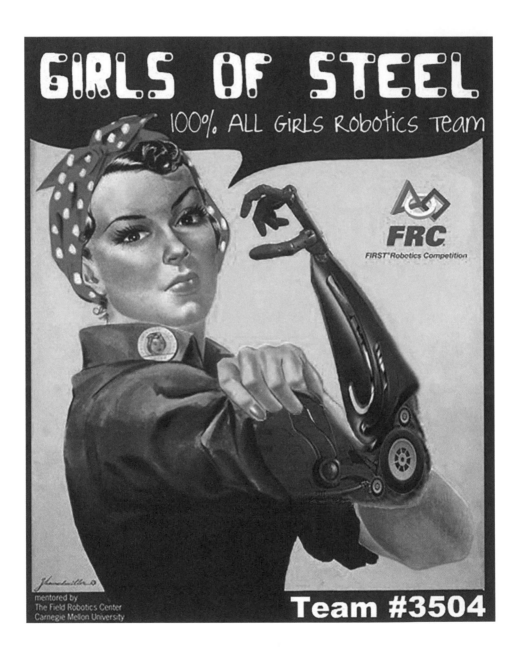

FORGET THE MAN OF STEEL
HERE ARE THE GIRLS OF STEEL

When working on the theme of error, it's easy to focus on the negative: the mishaps, mistakes and glitches of everything from the personal space of the mind to the vastness of the universe. But we thought we'd take some of the topics offered through error, and showcase something a little more positive.

Take, for example, robots. The mechanical fiction of this issue deals with them operating not-so-well, shall we say, but in America, robotics clubs are being used as a key way of getting young girls interested in STEM (Science, Technology, Engineering and Mathematics). Girls of Steel, an all-girls high school robotics team, is one such example.

"This programme is designed to empower and inspire girls," explains mentor Terry Richards. "The girls are the leaders, the designers, the builders, the programmers, the media specialists, the electronics experts – girls are in every role."

Girls of Steel, based in Pittsburgh and sponsored by the Field Robotics Centre at Carnegie Mellon University, brings together dozens of students from many schools, and is part of a larger organisation, FIRST (For Inspiration and Recognition in Science and Technology). Each year, FIRST presents a new challenge, and teams have six weeks to work together and build a robot. "After the six weeks there are competitions, which are basically like giant sporting events, just with 120-pound robots," explains one student, Lauren Scheller-Wolf.

"There are many skills and opportunities that the team get to tackle," continues Terry. "The girls learn a wide range of technical and business skills such as computer aided design (CAD), how to give presentations at conferences and outreach events, how to run social media, team leadership, electronics, programming, machining, mentoring at summer camps, and more. In addition they have unique opportunities such as meeting astronaut Cady Coleman via teleconference while she was on the International Space Station and again when she visited Pittsburgh, meeting former US Secretary of Education, Arne Duncan, meeting former US Secretary of State Hillary Clinton, meeting producers from Disney and inspiring the female characters in Big Hero 6, and more."

The opportunities and skills gained are incredible for young girls, but they're also teaching on a more personal level through the teamwork. "The obvious skills are technical, of course, but just as importantly, we are helping the girls find the confidence in themselves to lead, to choose their own path, and even to fail, get back up and try again," explains Thomas Pope, another mentor. "Being able to operate a milling machine, weld aluminium, or program a robot are all skills that may or may not be useful as they go off to college, but knowing

that they *can* do those things, that they can do anything they set their minds to doing … that I believe is the true value of the programme."

It's a sentiment shared by the students. On top of finding a confidence in several skillsets and team activities, it's helped broaden their potential career interests.

"When I began on the team I actually had no interest in STEM," says Langley Turcsanyi, a 10th grade student. "Being on the team not only gave me teamwork and leadership skills but also gave me more appreciation for the STEM field. Now looking at the news I see countless articles describing the newest and best inventions (including autonomous vehicles, etc) and I find it pretty amazing that a person came up with the incredible idea and then had the motivation to actually create it. There really is not any other field quite like STEM.

The Girls of Steel team

"Getting girls into the STEM world at a young age serves as a catalyst for their future. They realise that it is something that they can achieve and it gives them the motivation to do so."

This inspiration is teamed with a shift in cultural dialogue. Though there are still disparities in the number of females entering certain fields, the leaps in the last few years are clear, and teams like this are making a strong impact at possibly the most key age.

"For many years there was a stigma that girls couldn't do STEM," notes Lauren. "That they had to do the humanities and leave the hard sciences to the boys. This sprang from centuries of sexism; from ideas that girls were too delicate to do many things, that it would affect their ability to have children, that their minds just couldn't handle the strain. In a lot of ways this stigma is still around.

"Studies have shown that when girls and boys are little they like STEM in equal numbers, but once girls reach middle school the number of girls who say they're interested in STEM starts to decline sharply. I think a lot of the reason for this is that society tells girls in a million different ways (often unintentionally) that STEM isn't for them and that they're some sort of freak if they want to be a scientist or an engineer."

The need for role models comes up repeatedly from mentors and students alike. "I think there have been struggles with females focusing on their interests in STEM because of a lack of role models," notes Terry, pointing to the documentary *Miss Representation*, and Marian Wright Edelman's quote: "You can't be what you can't see."

But thanks to teams like theirs, young girls *can* see many examples of women across these fields, and get hands on experience in the process. On top of showcasing women in STEM to look up to, the team also makes the teens themselves role models to even younger girls, bridging the gap between being able to just showcase those far into their career, to also showing schoolgirls their peers doing wonderful things in tech.

Student Anne Kailin Northam explains, "Girls of Steel was formed with the goal of convincing every girl in the world that she can be part of a STEM field. Because of the stigma around girls in STEM and the fact that it is a male dominated field, girls are often discouraged even if they are interested. Our goal as a team is to exemplify female success to young girls and show them they can do anything."

Robotics is being used as a gateway to many things – career prospects, skills, teamwork, new friends – but most importantly, in the case of Girls of Steel, it's teaching a generation of young girls that limits do not exist and they can do anything, and what's more incredible than that?

You can find out more about Girls of Steel at girlsofsteelrobotics.com, or on Twitter: @TheGirlsOfSteel

ALMOST

ALMOST

MEET-CUTE

ALMOST A MEET-CUTE

JEN MCGREGOR

Waitress

I knew those new cups were a mistake. The minute I saw them stacked next to the espresso machine I thought *yup, those are going to be a disaster*. They're really wide, you see. More like really shallow soup bowls than cups. It's meant to be a statement or something. There are these stencils that fit over the cup with different seasonal messages, and we're meant to shake the cinnamon or chocolate or what have you in just the right way so that the message shows up. They gave us special training, if you can believe that. A whole morning just so we could all learn how to spell out 'Happy National Muffin Day!' or 'Happy Suicide Prevention Week!' or 'Happy International Dadaism Month!' in grains of cheap cooking chocolate.

The really cynical thing is that they didn't actually switch to these cups so they could pick out cutesy messages. They did it because a wide, shallow cup means the coffee has a greater surface area, which means it cools quicker, which means people drink their coffees faster, before they get cold, and order another. It's being passed off as some kind of artistic choice – complete with all these stupid prints of the new cups shot at weird, artsy angles all over the walls – when, actually, it's all about getting customers to buy more overpriced caffeine.

Anyway, the real problem is the saucers. Apparently whoever designed these sets missed the point of saucers. They're triangles. They're also a lot smaller than the cups, so there's enough room to put the complimentary biscotti bite on one of the points of the triangle, but there's nowhere to balance the spoon or the serviette when you're carrying the coffee. And of course, it doesn't catch drips. So you're carrying this wide, shallow cup that's apparently been designed to slop coffee over the side, and the only place it can go is straight onto whatever's underneath. Like the floor. Or a customer.

And that's what happened. I knew it. I *knew* it would happen to somebody. I was just … really hoping it wasn't going to be me. And that if it was, it wouldn't be *her*.

Oh, god …

OK, let me tell you why this was a disaster and why it's so stupid. I don't even know this guy's name, right? She's just this guy who comes in here most days, mid-afternoon, right before the end of my shift, and it's the highlight of my day. Believe me, when you're on the opening shift every day and you're dealing with the morning caffeine rush and the lunch rush and the general crapness of coffee-lovers, you need a highlight. She comes in for about half an hour, forty-five minutes each day, and she sits on her own and reads while she has lunch. She orders a different sand-wich each day, never the same thing two days in a row, but there's one thing about her order that never changes – *she never orders coffee*. Ever. And you have no idea how much I love that about her. The only hot drink I've ever seen her order is an Earl Grey tea. And she takes it black, medium strength, always takes the teabag out before the bergamot gets overwhelming. While it's still delicate. Coffee is never delicate. Coffee is just blunt force trauma in a cup.

I've been working up the courage to talk to her for weeks now. Not to ask her out, not at this stage, but just to get a conversation going. I just don't know what to say. It used to be so easy with people who hang around coffee shops, I'd just look for the people who were reading books I like and start chatting about them. If someone likes the same books as you they're worth investigating, right? But this girl, she has a Kindle or an iPad or something – it's in a case, so I can't see exactly what it is and I have no idea what she's reading. And just walking up and saying "What are you reading?" seems too invasive, so for ages now I've been trying to think of something else, anything else, to give me a way in.

And today I thought I had it. This morning I looked at those ridiculous stencils and thought I could actually be grateful to them for once. 'Happy National Book Lovers Day', it said. And I thought *Yes! That's it! I can be so casual about this. All I need to do is say "seems appropriate" or something like that and I'm in! Conversation started!* It didn't even matter that she doesn't drink coffee, I decided I would comp her a cupcake and pick out the message in chocolate on the plate. Sorted.

Then … the cups. Those … ridiculous cups. I was taking an order to the table next to hers, cappuccino in each hand. The cupcake I'd chosen for her was sitting at the prep station with the stencilling already done, ready to be served next. Then … I don't know. I slipped. I fell. As I steadied myself I watched this mini-tsunami of coffee rise and swell and crash over the side of the cup in my left hand, and I stuck my hand out hoping that I could somehow catch the drops as they fell, but instead I sent an aftershock across the cup and even more cappuccino surged over the edge. There was nothing I could do.

And I looked at her, sitting right underneath where my hand had been. Her coat … it was pale grey wool. And the coffee … And the look on her face, just shocked …

And that's why I'm handing in my notice. I can't …

I can't.

NOT HAVING

A GIRAFFE

NOT HAVING A GIRAFFE

PICKLISH

I walked past them every day, making sure that I walk between mother and calf, stare up at them and give them voices, usually some sort of question that the wee one asks the big one. Sometimes it's about the plains, or the lions, other times about the trees or the fighting with necks. But it's an inquisitive wee dude, at least, so it seems in my mind.

They've taken on a life of their own in my head though I often wonder what they think of the latest shite blockbuster on at the tragically misnamed Omni Centre, or the streams of idiots coming out of John Lewis clutching their always knowingly oversold pish. I feel sorry about the fact that they can never turn their heads and look down Leith Walk to the sea. It's a wee shame, so it is.

So I decided that I needed to do something about it. Animal liberation, ken? I mean, I do know that they aren't really animals, just sculptures, but it's just the way that the wee one looks at the big one. Yearning, like. Inquisitive. It's no fair that they should just be stuck there like that. It's no.

So I came up with a plan. Took ages, like. A real labour of love. But the things you'll do when you know that the right thing needs to be done, eh? I photographed them from loads of angles, figured out their heights and estimated their weights.

I spent hours looking at the work of a company called Boston Dynamics. That and reading up on welding and things like mechanical degrees of freedom. I watched videos of giraffes on YouTube, pressing pause-play-pause-play over and over to try and figure them out.

I had to do it quickly, all in a couple of hours at the most. I bought hi-viz clothes and a workie type windshield, and cordoned off the areas around the giraffe's legs, ready to give the excuse Banksy suggested. That is: if anyone asked what I was doing then to simply complain about working conditions.

It was 2am on a clear Tuesday morning in September. I told myself that I probably had until 5am. I got to work, setting up scaffolding around them, making sure they were held in place before I chopped off their legs below the knees. I inserted a couple of car batteries into their hollow bodies to power the servos that were going to drive the hinges that I was installing between their femurs and tibias.

They needed a wee splint down their legs with a channel cut out, in order to maintain vertical motion, but I knew it was a small price to pay for freedom. I'm sure the wee one even winked at me, but it had been a long few days not sleeping much. The Modafinil had kept me pepped. Perhaps too much, but I'd be able to sleep easy once more once my task was complete.

I managed to lever them out of the concrete, it felt like the mother had even lifted her leg to help. I supplied them with flat shoes to help their balance. Leith Walk is a steep street and they had a mile of running before they would reach the shore. I attached an Arduino microcontroller that would tell the servos when to move what leg at which time. I shuffled them around to face north. We were ready.

They sprung into life the second I attached the final cable and horsed it down the road. The sun was just rising, and a few hardy souls were making the trip into work, probably unsure if they were still dreaming. I tore after them, barely able to keep up, panting, exhausted but deliriously overjoyed at the spark of life and happiness I had given to these caged beasts.

Suddenly, tragedy struck near Albert Street; the mother careered into the number 22, toppling both bus and beast. I slowed down for a second, a moment of respect for the fallen, before racing after the wee guy. It was all about him. I could hear what I imagined was the mother's roar behind me, encouraging him onwards.

We were approaching the bottom of Leith Walk and I was breathing oot ma arse, when I saw a police car turn the corner from Constitution Street. The wee guy had reared up on his hind legs, from clipping a bump in the road. He came crashing down right into the car's windscreen. It wasn't supposed to end like this. He never made it. I had to go. I had to get out of here. No one would understand that what I had done was an act of liberation, they'd just call it criminal damage or some such. Perhaps even culpable homicide. I wasn't sticking around to find out. I jumped on the number 35 that took me all the way to the airport. I thought South Africa at first, but then Zimbabwe probably don't have an extradition treaty with the UK.

I bet I can free some more giraffes there too.

WILLKOMMEN

DHACHAIGH

WILLKOMMEN DHACHAIGH

ROBBIE MACLEÒID

Air ùr-dhùsgadh o mo norrag làitheil (eadar 2f agus 4f), agus a' sealltainn a-mach dorsan Tyrellan Heights gu dealbh glas an latha, cha tàinig sìon sam bith a-steach orm. Bha uair a thìde agam airson m' fhiaclan a ghlanadh agus a dhèanamh boillsgeach, m' fhalt a chàradh, agus mo ghàire airson an latha fheuchainn. Thòisicheadh iad a' nochdadh às dèidh 5f, an toiseach mar bhoinneagan, ach gu slaodach a' tighinn nan sruth. Agus tha mi eòlach air gach aon dhiubh.

5.01f, nochdadh Àireamh a h-Aon, fear àrd tana caol, aodann tana, tana, tana. Bhiodh màileid aige gach latha den t-seachdain, agus bhithinn a' tomhas dè bha na broinn gach latha. Diluain 's dòcha gur e na foirmean a bh' aige airson cuideigineach o thall thairis, nach biodh san dùthaich ach airson latha a-mhàin, agus bha e fo chùram air eagal 's nach robh na foirmean air an eadar-theangachadh gu ceart. Dimàirt 's dòcha gur e dealbhan a rinn a nighean dha, is i ga ionndrainn on a ghluais e a-steach an seo. Dihaoine 's dòcha gur e foirmean airson cur às dha còmhnaidh aig Tyrellan Heights – no duilleag airson fàgail às dèidh dha cur às dha fhèin. Dè bha dol air cùl nan sùilean dubha ud? Chruthaichinn beachd ùr gach latha dha, mar thiodhlac, ged nach do mhothaich e a-riamh. "Willkommen dhachaigh." Ghnogadh e cheann nuair a chanainn sin, ach cha shealladh e orm.

5.04f thilleadh Àireamh a Dhà. Tè inntinneach a th' innte, is i an-còmhnaidh a' cabadaich. O, chan ann riumsa, fhios 'ad, chan ann, chan ann, chan ann. Ach bhon a thig i tron doras gloinne ud gus an àm a tha dorsan an àrdaicheir a' dùnadh, bidh i a' bruidhinn, mar gum biodh caraid còmhla rithe. Nach eil sin àraid? Feumaidh gu bheil aon de na rudan ud aice na cluais, no na beul, fhios agad? Na creutairean àraid ud. Chan fhaca mi a-riamh gàire air a h-aghaidh ach a' ghàire bheag a dhèanadh i riumsa fhad 's a bha i a' bruidhinn. Mar gum b' e caraid dhomh a bh' innte, agus gun robh i eòlach orm, agus gun robh i duilich gun robh ge bith cò ris a bha i a' bruidhinn a' cur bacadh air ar còmhradh fhìn.

A-nis, às dèidh Àireamh a Dhà tha beàrn mhòr ann – cha bhi duine a' nochdadh airson sia mionaidean.

21

Eòlach air gach aon dhiubh. Chan ann air an ainmean, seadh, aidichidh mi sin, ach gu dè am feum a th' ann an eòlas ainmean? Eòlas anmannan a tha nas cudromaiche. Chan eil fhios acasan idir air m' ainm-sa, ach chan eil sin a' ciallachadh nach eil iad eòlach orm, a bheil? (Chan eil!)

Co-dhiù, aig 5.10f nochdadh Àireamh a Trì. Chan eil fhios nach robh esan uair dèidheil air an deoch, no na dathan no rudeigin den leithid, oir bha a shùilean lom. Chan eil mi a' ciallachadh gun robh coltas ann gun robh e an-còmhnaidh a' sealltainn air rudeigin fad às, tha mi a' ciallachadh nach robh ach geal na shùilean, fhios 'ad, mar a chithear le muinntir na dibhe. Co-dhiù, shealladh e orm nuair a chanainn "Willkommen dhachaigh" ris – uill, shaoilinn gun robh e a' coimhead orm, fhios 'ad, ach tha e duilich a ràdh leis nach robh pongan beaga dubha aige na shùilean. Cha nochdadh gàire no bròn air aodann; shealladh e orm, choisicheadh e seachad, bheireadh e air putan an àrdaicheir, dh'fhosgladh na dorsan agus dheidheadh e à sealladh.

Tha cuid de dhaoine nas càileire na feadhainn eile.

A' tilleadh gu ainmean, saoil a bheil iad air ainm a thoirt ormsa, nan inntinn is nan eanchainn? Saoil a bheil ainm eadar-dhealaichte aig gach aon dhiubh ormsa? 'S dòcha gur e "An Neach Fàilte" a th' aig Àireamh a h-Aon orm. 'S dòcha "Fear an Taighe" no "Bean an Dorais" a th' aig Àireamh a Dhà orm. No 's dòcha nach eilear ach a' smaointinn orm mar seo: "Willkommen dhachaigh".

'S e 5.13f an turas mu dheireadh a bhios neach a' tighinn a-steach na aonar – às dèidh sin 's e dithistean is triùirean is fiù 's ceathrar no dhà a bhios a' tighinn a-steach. Agus, na togaibh seo ceàrr, a dhaoine a tha an-còmhnaidh ann an triùirean no ceathraran, ach chan eil mi idir a' faireachdainn cho faisg air na daoine sin is a tha mi air an fheadhainn a bhios a' tighinn a-steach nan aonar. Ma dh'fhaodte gur ann leis nach bi na dithistean agus na triùirean an-còmhnaidh a' dèanamh an aon rud gach latha – ag amannan, bidh iad ri gàire, amannan eile ri còmhradh, amannan eile a' strì. Agus tha seo fìor, tha, ged nach creideadh tu e – chunnaic mi dithist agus bha iad a' cur am bilean ri chèile. Nach eil sin àraid? Agus bha an gàirdeanan air a chèile cuideachd, tha sin dìreach gòrach. Tric 's e an dithist ud a bhios a' tighinn aig 5.43f, fhios 'ad, Àireamh Ceathrad 's a h-Aon agus Àireamh Ceathrad 's a Dhà, a th' annta. Innsidh mi seo dhuibh, ach na canaibh guth ri taibhse, tha mi air tòiseachadh air smaointinn orra mar "An Dithist Amadan" an àite Àireamh Ceathrad 's a h-Aon agus Àireamh Ceathrad 's a Dhà! Ach chan eil sin ceart, chan eil idir. Àireamh Ceathrad 's a h-Aon agus Àireamh Ceathrad 's a Dhà a th' annta gu ceart, fhios 'ad.

Bidh Àireamh a h-Aon-Deug agus Àireamh a Trì-Deug a' tighinn a-steach aig amannan eadar-dhealaichte, le buidhnean eadar-dhealaichte, ach tha mi cinnteach gu bheil an aon fhàileadh orra. Nach eil sin àraid cuideachd? Chan eil mi gus cus ùine a chosg orra ge-tà, nuair a tha fhathast Àireamhan Aon gu Ceithir cho inntinneach. Saoil dè dìreach a th' ann am màileid Àireimh a h-Aon. Dòchas? Breisleach?

Co-dhiù, aig 5.13f bidh Àireamh a Ceithir a' nochdadh. Chan urrainn dhomh cuimhneachadh buileach dè an coltas a th' air (a th' oirre?), ach nuair a chì mi e no i gach latha tha mi a' cuimhneachadh, agus ciamar a b' urrainn dhomh a dhìochuimhneachadh?

Aon latha, bidh an t-airgead agam àite a ghlèidheadh dhomh fhìn ann an Tyrellan Heights. Choisichinn a-steach gach latha aig 5.07f, gus am biodh gach nì rèidh is cothromach. Bu chòir do chuideigin tighinn aig 5.07f, fhios 'ad. Bidh aig 5.01f, 5.04f, [5.07f], 5.10f, 5.13f, mar sin tha còir aig cuideigineach tighinn aig 5.07f, cuideigin a' tilleadh dhachaigh, cudeigin is carson nach bu mhise a bhiodh ann?

Agus chanadh cuideigin eile na faclan seasmhach, daingeann ud riumsa.

Uill, co-dhiù, 's fheudar dhomh bhith tilleadh dhan leabaidh. Chan eil feum orm gu 7m air làrna mhàireach airson suidhe is gan coimhead uile a' fàgail son an latha, gach latha, 7–9m, mar is càilear, mar is taitneach. Chan eil faclan agam anns a' mhadainn ge-tà, chan eil faclan a dhìth, tha mi ann mar phongan a dh'aithnicheas iad, fhios 'ad. Caillidh mi mo bhriathran sa mhadainn, ach tha iad an-còmhnaidh gam fheitheamh nuair a dhùisgeas mi aig 1f, mar charaid cunbhalach còir.

Tha mi smaointinn gu bheil eagal orm, ach chan eil mi cinnteach. Mas e 's gu bheil, bidh e leis nach eil feum agam ach air dà fhacal a-mhàin – 'Willkommen' agus 'dhachaigh'. Tha eagal orm, mas e 's gu bheil, agus chan eil mi cinnteach a bheil, fhios 'ad, ach mas e 's gu bheil, tha eagal orm gun ionnsaich iad gu bheil barrachd na dà fhacal agam nam eanchainn, is gum bi mi air an fheasgar mar a tha mi air madainn, fhios 'ad, gun fhaclan, uill, gun fhaclan ach na dhà:

"Willkommen dhachaigh."

Na faclan reusanta, daingeann, seasmhach ud.

"Willkommen dhachaigh."

Chan eil e dèanamh ciall ma-thà, mas e 's gu bheil eagal orm, gu bheil mi a' cantainn na h-aona h-abairt rium fhèin gach oidhche mus tèid mi a-steach dhan leabaidh: "Oidhche mhath a charaid."

Agus an uair sin, air oir a' bhruadair:

"Willkommen dhachaigh."

WILLKOMMEN HOME

ROBBIE MACLEOD

Freshly awake from my daily nap (between 2pm and 4pm), and looking out the doors of Tyrellan Heights at the grey appearance of the day, no thoughts came into my mind. I had an hour to brush my teeth and make them shine, to sort my hair, and to practise my smile for the day. They would start appearing after 5pm, at first like little droplets, but slowly they would become a current. And I know every one of them.

5.01pm, Number One would appear, a tall thin slender man, with a very thin, thin face. He would have a briefcase every day of the week, and every day I would guess what was inside it. Monday, it might be forms for someone from abroad, only in the country for a day, and he was worried in case the forms weren't translated properly. Tuesday, perhaps it was pictures that his daughter had drawn for him, because she missed him since he had moved in here. Friday, it might be forms to stop people living at Tyrellan Heights – or a note to leave behind after committing suicide. What went on behind those black eyes? I would come up with a new idea each day for him, like a present, though he never noticed. 'Willkommen home.' He would nod his head when I said that, but he wouldn't look at me.

5.04pm, Number Two would return. She's an interesting woman, always chatting. Oh, not to me, you know, oh no, no, no. But when she comes through that glass door until when the doors of the lift close, she speaks away, as if she had a friend with her. Isn't that peculiar? She must have one of those things in her ear, or in her mouth, you know? Those strange contraptions. I never saw a smile on her face except the small smile she would give me when she is speaking. As if I were her friend, and that she knew me, and that she was sorry that whoever it was she was speaking to had prevented our own conversation.

Now, after Number Two there is a large gap – no-one appears for six minutes.

I know every one of them. Not their names, yeah, I'll admit that, but what's the use in knowing names? It's knowing the souls that's more important. They don't know my name at all, but that doesn't mean that they don't know me, does it? (No, it doesn't!)

Anyway, at 5.10pm Number Three would appear. I'm not sure if he was once overly fond of the drink, or colours, or something like that, because his eyes were bare. I don't mean that it appeared like he was always looking at something far away, I mean that there was only white in his eyes, you know, like what you see with people who are heavy on the drink. Anyway, he would look at me when I'd say 'Willkommen home' to him – well, I'd think he was looking at me, you know, but it's difficult to tell since he didn't have little black dots in his eyes. He would neither smile or look sad; he would look at me, walk past, press the button for the lift, the doors would open, and he would go out of sight.

Some people are more pleasant than others.

Going back to names, do you think they've given me a name, in their minds, in their heads? Do you think each of them has a different name for me? Maybe I'm the 'Welcomer' to Number One. Perhaps I'm the 'House Man' or the 'Door Woman' to Number Two. Or maybe I'm only thought of like this: 'Willkommen home'.

5.13pm is the last time that someone comes in on their own – after that it's groups of two and three and even one or two groups of four that come in. Now, don't take this the wrong way, you people that are always in threes or fours, but I don't feel at all as close to those people as I do to the ones that come in on their own. Maybe it's because the groups of two and three aren't always doing the same thing every day – at times they'll be laughing, other times conversing, other times squabbling. And this is true, it is, even though you wouldn't believe it – I once saw two people and they were putting their lips together. Isn't that strange? And their arms were over each other as well, it's just foolish. Frequently it's those two that come at 5.43pm, you know, Number Forty-One and Number Forty-Two. I'll tell you this, but don't tell a soul, I've started thinking of them as 'The Two Idiots' instead of Number Forty-One and Forty-Two! But that's not right, not at all. They are – you know, properly – Number Forty-One and Number Forty-Two.

Number Eleven and Number Thirteen come in at different times, with different groups, but I'm certain that they have the same smell. Isn't that peculiar as well? I'm not going to spend too much time on them though, since Numbers One to Four are so interesting. Just think what could be in Number One's briefcase. Hope? Delirium?

Anyway, at 5.13pm Number Four appears. I can never quite remember what he (she?) looks like, but when I see him or her, I remember, and how could I forget?

One day, I'll have the money to get myself a place in Tyrellan Heights. I would walk in each day at 5.07pm, so that everything would be right and proper. Someone should come in at 5.07pm, you know. They do at 5.01pm, 5.04pm,

[5.07pm], 5.10pm, 5.13pm, so someone should come at 5.07pm, someone returning home, someone, and why shouldn't it be me?

And someone else would say those solid, steady words to me.

Well, anyway, I need to get back to bed. I'm not needed until 7am tomorrow morning, to sit and to watch them all leave for the day, every day, 7–9am, as is pleasant and nice. I don't have any words in the morning though, no words are needed, I am there like musical notes that they recognise, you know. I lose my words in the morning, but they're always waiting for me when I wake up at 4pm, like a kind and constant friend.

I think I'm afraid, but I'm not sure. If I am, it will be because I only ever need two words – 'Willkommen' and 'home'. I'm afraid, if I actually am afraid, and I'm not sure I am, you know, but if I am afraid, it's that they might find out that I have more than two words in my head, and in the evenings I'll be just like as I am in the mornings, you know, without any words, well, without any words except two:

'Willkommen home.'

Those sensible, solid, steady words.

'Willkommen home.'

Though if I am actually afraid, it doesn't make sense that I say the same phrase to myself each night before I get into bed: 'Good night, my friend.'

And then, on the edge of dreaming:

'Willkommen home.'

DON'T MISTAKE YOURSELF FOR JOAN OF ARC

DON'T MISTAKE YOURSELF FOR JOAN OF ARC

ALICE TARBUCK

You've had enough:
'enough' here meaning several of an ABV of 8%, 'enough'
a rough 12g torqueing through the stomach lining into blood,
until the line of boys sways,
your breath the same fast rising breath that stands
inordinately small before a king, to tell the truth of something in the air which
speaks unbidden. Glass in the thumb from a cracked phone screen
blood on the scarlet dancing girl emoji/skin fleck on the flame emoji
that's the bit they all like best.

The Virgin Orleans
crouches under the skull, the pilot light flares first green, then blue
and the Archangel Michael is leisurely turning away
decked in the black and white of bouncers everywhere,
his Bluetooth headset blinking, his eyes not anywhere when she is marched,
triumphal d'Arc, out to the shining pavement, or off to Compeigne.

Curl up in the space of suffering, claim the scorch of ground
now tarmacked over. Lineate the crackle of her burning,
locate at the white heart of it your own, live, heart
but don't cut and paste her eyes with yours. Remember that she spoke
with tongues, peeled a Compeed patch and then kept dancing,
lent a tampon, comprehend that she was
nineteen and mardy, that the jeer of men was as loud
as thousands of struck matches, that their hands and arms
tied ropes and stacked up wood. Are you sure, now, that you
can see in her yourself? It is a better view than looking down
in the taxi, flexing your hands and wondering
about the beauty of the flames from the expensive seats.

SPINNERS OF AIR

SPINNERS OF AIR

ALI GEORGE

Elizabeth found the spinning wheel by mistake.

She was supposed to be helping her mother-in-law look for bits and pieces to do up for eBay, but she'd snuck off into the depths of the jumble for a few moments of quiet and wandered off the beaten path. Finally, she'd ended up at the very edge of the church hall, next to a shoogling pile of detritus primed to topple at any moment. Most of it looked to be broken.

Elizabeth's mother-in-law didn't like to fix broken things. She was a 'sponge a bit of paint across an elderly coffee table and attach a hefty mark up' kind of a person. Elizabeth, though, considered herself a fixer.

The pile was about eleven feet tall and featured three-legged chairs, a suite of kitchen cupboards with the doors hanging off, and some wonky shelves. As she looked more closely, she saw the ancient spinning wheel at the centre, forming an integral structural support.

She'd never seen a spinning wheel in person, so she couldn't tell what was wrong with it exactly, but she was sure it could be mended. More importantly, she knew she wanted it in her life.

Elizabeth cast her eyes about for the owner of the pile. Most shoppers seemed to be avoiding this particular corner, walled in on all sides by an antique bookseller, a young woman with a vintage dress rack, and an elderly man giving tarot readings. They all had their backs to her.

"Excuse me," Elizabeth said to nobody in particular. "I'd like to buy that spinning wheel?"

"That'll be £25," came a voice from within the tower. No, not within it. Behind it. There was a gap on the other side. That meant the whole lot must be free-standing. Instinctively Elizabeth took a step backwards as the owner of the voice – a tiny old woman who looked a bit like a conker – maneuvered the wheel out from the base of the junk pile.

"It's a bit shonky," the woman said, "but it's fixable if you can be bothered. I couldn't, myself. Not with my rickets being what it is."

Elizabeth smiled politely and handed over the cash, wondering how rickets impacted on fixing a spinning wheel, but slightly afraid to ask. Her mother-in-law would be looking for her by now, and she'd have to explain that she'd gone off-piste. Being caught red-handed listening to a story from a strange old lady would only add to an already lengthy list of transgressions.

As she went in search of her shopping companion, the wheel clamped awkwardly under her arm, she didn't notice the old lady slip out of the side door of the church hall, never to be seen again.

* * *

"Look at this," Elizabeth called. "I can get it fixed at the Bonnington Industrial Museum. That's not far from here, is it?"

"I guess," Tom grunted from the depths of the kitchen. He wasn't interested in museums at the best of times, and at that moment was engaged in the creation of a particularly complicated soufflé.

"Can we go?" she asked.

"I guess."

She smiled to herself. When she had moved down here, she'd been surprised to learn that in Tom's five years in the city he'd never been to a single museum, much less all the outlying collections housed in random cottages around the county. The Bonnington Industrial Museum turned out to be one of the latter. In fact, it didn't even have the whole of the random cottage to itself. It was just a room in a house that had once belonged to some weavers. The woman behind the counter was full of knowledge though, and her eyes lit up when she saw the broken spinning wheel.

Her excitement, she explained, came from the fact that most of the young people these days aren't interested in spinning, weaving, or other traditional crafts. In her experience, the ones who did knit or crochet tended to go and buy synthetic wool from the pound shop. Elizabeth smiled politely and decided not to mention her most recent project, an army of sparky mouse finger puppets made from just such offending materials.

The excitable curator told them to have a wander round the museum whilst she took the wheel through to her colleague in the back room. With that, she pushed a photocopied factsheet across the counter and vanished through a green velvet curtain into the unknown.

Tom picked up the paper and peered at it. The print was tiny. Whoever had made it wanted visitors to get as much information from their stay as was humanly possible.

"There's a loom in a shed out the back," he announced, "and in here there's textiles, some furniture very like some that might once have belonged to some weavers, and some advertising for the new mill which put them all out of business. It's going to be a rollercoaster ride."

They picked their way around the tiny room as slowly as they could, politely reading every placard and sign they could find. It wasn't a very good museum, but they could hardly say so when the staff were within earshot.

"Done!" trilled the curator, making them jump. "But now you really must learn to use it – did you know we have a spinning group here?"

Elizabeth studiously avoided Tom's gaze. "No!" she lied, "how wonderful."

"Well, we do," the curator replied. "They meet at 3pm on Sundays, so you're just in time. Look, here's Maxine now. She's in charge."

Maxine was short and stout and had very curly grey hair. At the mention of her name, she put down the spinning wheel she'd had slung over her shoulder, and fumbled in her shirt pocket for a pair of gold-framed glasses. She proceeded to look the both of them up and down over the top of them, before sticking out a hand for Elizabeth to shake.

"We meet upstairs," she said. "Come on, I'll show you."

"I'll just go for a walk, then," Tom said. His voice was tight. "Give me a ring when you're done."

She shot an apologetic look. "Thanks," she called, but he was already gone.

Maxine led her up creaking stairs to a long room with low, sloping ceilings. There was a semi circle of stools at one end, and a stack of wicker baskets. Maxine parked her spinning wheel next to one of the stools and motioned Elizabeth to do the same. She picked up two baskets, then pulled out an enormous plastic bag of fluffy wool.

"I don't suppose you have your own?" she asked.

Elizabeth shook her head. "I didn't know I was coming."

"Liar," Maxine said. "People always know they're coming."

"We-ell," Elizabeth conceded, "I wanted to. But the wheel was broken and I didn't know whether it would be fixed in time."

Maxine pulled a fuzzy rope of wool from the bag. "Here," she said, "use this. Have you ever spun before?"

She didn't wait for an answer. Elizabeth watched with furrowed brow as she wound a length of wool she'd spun earlier around the bobbin, deftly threading it through the guiding hooks, then loosened the unspun fibres before winding the two together. She was so engrossed in following the movement of the other woman's hands and feet she barely noticed the other members of the group filing into the room.

"Here," Maxine said, "your go."

When she was happy Elizabeth had got the hang of it enough not to spin her own hair, or prick herself and fall into a coma, Maxine settled behind her own wheel. They fell into a comfortable clack-clacking rhythm, and it was some time before

Elizabeth looked up from what she was doing to examine the rest of the room.

There were seven spinners altogether. Those who had come in after her and Maxine seemed to be whispering to each other, but they stopped when she caught their eyes.

"I'm Elizabeth," she said at last, hoping this might defuse the tension in the room. Perhaps they weren't used to having strangers at the group, in which case the best remedy was an introduction.

"We are the Spinners of Air," said the man sitting across from her on the other end of the crescent of stools. He had very dark skin, a shiny bald head, and a serious expression on his face.

"You mean, like the River Aire?" she asked. It ran quite nearby. She'd swotted up on local knowledge before moving there with Tom. All that trivia made her an invaluable member of the pub quiz team.

The man was shaking his head, though. "No," he said. "Not like the river. The element."

She snuck a glance around the rest of the group to see if he was making fun of her. None of them were smirking, or shaking their head in disapproval about a joke at her expense.

"Tell her about the strangest thing you've ever spun, Gary," said a woman with a waist length braid of red hair. She was rosy-cheeked, and sat carding wool with two big brushes, slapping them together a little too aggressively for Elizabeth's liking.

"You first, Caroline," he said. "What was it you told us last week? You spun enough human hair to make a cardigan?"

"I made the cardigan too," Caroline said proudly. "Sold it on my Etsy shop for fifty quid. I told 'em it was mohair."

Elizabeth tried not to look appalled.

"I've spun fire," piped up the person on Caroline's right, who was mostly covered by a multicoloured poncho with an enormous hood.

"Shut up, Storm, you haven't spun fire," squeaked the person to Caroline's left.

"Have too."

"Have not."

"Have too."

"Have not."

"Have!"

"Haven't!"

"ENOUGH!" Caroline thundered, and the two of them sulkily returned to their spinning.

"They're twins," Caroline said apologetically, as if that explained anything.

Throughout all this, the sixth woman had sat in silence with her hands folded in her lap. The spinning wheel in front of her was black. she was dressed in black, and with shiny black hair that hung to her shoulders. The overall effect was to make her already pale skin look even paler, almost translucent.

"How about you, Soo?" Maxine asked. "What's the strangest thing you've ever spun?"

A strange smile softened her mouth. For a long few moments, Elizabeth thought she wouldn't say anything at all – but then she spoke. Slowly, deliberately, thinking carefully about each word to make herself understood in a second language.

"I have spun Time," she told them.

There was a burst of laughter from the twins, who got a furious look from their mother for their trouble. "I call bullshit," Storm said, when they had recovered themselves.

"It is not bullshit," Soo replied cheerfully. "It is fact. I have to concentrate hard to do it, but I can. I could teach you, if I chose…" She paused, giving the rest of the group a significant look. "But I won't. It is dangerous. After all, I can pull out a thread from the air around you and spin it so tight that your whole self would begin to unravel. I have destroyed many lives in this way. Cities, also."

"Don't be daft," Maxine said. 'How would you even start winding time around your bobbin?'

Soo did not answer this in words. She merely smiled enigmatically, and put her right hand in the air as though she was feeling about for something.

"That's how you spin air," Gary said, but he was silenced by a look from Soo. She was rubbing her thumb and index finger together now, as though there were something gripped between them.

Apparently satisfied she had what she wanted, Soo made the motion of tying something to the bobbin, and then began to operate her wheel. Unlike the others, it spun without a sound. What was it made of? Elizabeth wondered. It was so black and shiny and smooth – could it be ebony? It didn't seem like wood, somehow. It reminded her of stone, like obsidian.

Soo's face was animated as she worked, apparently spinning something, though none of them could see what it was. They felt the air begin to cool though, and each of them noticed a curious sensation that everything seemed to be going into slow motion. Then quite suddenly everything sped up and went much too fast.

Elizabeth found herself downstairs in the museum, in the car with Tom, at home in the flat, at the church hall surrounded by jumble.

"Found anything good?" asked her mother-in-law from behind an enormous pile of broken looking furniture.

Elizabeth stared at her in shock, but couldn't work out why she was surprised to see her. They had come here together, after all. They went to the church hall every other Saturday, looking for jumble that could be done up for eBay.

"No," she said, feeling sad although she wasn't sure why.

"Nothing's caught my eye."

THE DRAWING PROCESS

DEENA E. JACOBS

THE
UNIVERSE FACTORY

THE UNIVERSE FACTORY

CHRIS MCQUEER

Tam got up from his desk. He needed a break from staring at the screen or he was going to scream. He navigated through the maze of desks to the staffroom, walked over to the meal fabricator. The small silver machine scanned his ID badge and greeted him in a gruff Scottish accent. Tam heard everybody speaking in Scottish accents, thanks to the translator he had implanted in his brain, so he could understand his colleagues.

"Awrite, Tam?" the meal fabricator said. "Yer no scheduled fur yer break for another hour."

"I know, I know. I just have a bit of a creative block just now," Tam said, rubbing the back of his neck.

"Happens tae the best of us, my man. Anyway, wit ye having? Fancy trying something new? I've just downloaded an update that gives me access tae aw the food and drink fae the Bode's Galaxy." The display panel of the machine lit up and displayed a GIF of a winking man. "Go on, Tam. How aboot a nice big bowl of polyps?" The screen changed to show Tam exactly what a bowl of polyps looked like. He declined the machine's offer.

"Eh, naw. I'll just have a cup a coffee please," Tam said.

"Fair enough," said the machine and a Styrofoam cup full of hot brown liquid materialised on the tray for Tam to collect. Tam mumbled a "cheers" and walked away. The machine displayed a GIF of a cartoon dog watching from a window as his owner drove away.

Back at his desk, Tam sipped the scalding hot coffee and burnt his tongue. "Fuck thake," he said under his breath.

"Everything okay, Tam?" asked Frigo the Rectoid, an eight-foot-tall, two-dimensional, black rectangle. His accent was more of a well-to-do Edinburgh as opposed to the rough Glaswegian of the meal fabricator.

"Aye fine, Frigo. Just struggling to come up wi ideas," Tam said, letting out an exasperated sigh. He moved his mouse to deactivate the screensaver on his computer. The same computer he had used back on Earth when he was an architect, only now it was running software that was infinitely more powerful

41

than the simple drawing programs he had once used. Tam used to design build-ings, now he designed parallel universes. The brightest, most creative minds in the universe ended up here, at the Universe Factory. A large, grey office building orbiting a black hole in the most remote, inaccessible region of space. Humans generally weren't suited to the job due to their own vanity. The first human universe creator became obsessed with watching the alternate versions of himself go about their lives. He ended up being sacked after a fortnight. Tam, however, had been in the job for seven years now and had been enjoying up until now. He was running out of ideas.

A picture of Earth filled the screen of Tam's computer. He rotated it and zoomed in and out, hoping some inspiration would come to him, but it didn't. Tam usually had a wealth of ideas for other versions of Earth to insert into his parallel universes but today he had drawn a blank. *Adding in a third gender? Naw, already done that. Fish fly in the air and birds swim in the sea? Naw, that would be too weird. A world where humans never discovered electricity? Hmmm, maybe. Naw, wait, disnae matter. Tried that two year ago. Disaster. Why is this so fucking hard, man?* There was literally an infinite amount of possibilities and he couldn't think of a single one. He lifted his coffee to his mouth again then placed it back on the desk, it was still too hot. He turned to Frigo to see what he was working on. Frigo was invisible when viewed from side-on.

"Frigo?" Tam said. Frigo turned to face him. The deep darkness had unsettled Tam from the moment he first lay eyes on the machine. It was even darker than the centre of the black hole outside the window. "What you working on?"

"This," Frigo floated a tiny hologram galaxy over to Tam's side of the desk.

"Cool," Tam waved his hands around the hologram, causing it to meander through the air. Even after seven years in space, he was still fascinated by alien technology.

"That's a new version of the Milky Way galaxy, where you're from. With a new version of Earth since you can't come up with anything half-decent," Frigo boomed.

"What's different about it?" Tam asked.

"You're not an ugly bastard in this version, hahaha!"

"Aw get it up ye," Tam said. He batted the hologram away from him and back over to Frigo. The tiny galaxy was absorbed into Frigo's body. He turned to the side again, disappearing from view. He continued to laugh at his own joke.

Tam lowered his head on to his desk. The coolness of the table against his forehead calmed him. He sat like that for a couple of minutes and for those few moments he was back on Earth. He was sitting in his office in Partick; the low hum of printers in the background, the constant sound of measurements being recited floating through the air, the rhythmic clicking of mouses. These sounds always stimulated Tam back on Earth and hearing them again, if only in his imagination, caused ideas to pour into Tam's mind.

"Tam!" a shrill voice brought him back to the Universe Factory in an instant. It was Clerisso, his boss. She was a small humanoid creature, no bigger than a pint glass, from a dwarf planet in the Andromeda Galaxy. She buzzed around Tam's head, her tiny wings beating so fast they were almost invisible. "I believe you have work to be doing? I don't seem to recall asking you to have a wee rest."

"Sorry, Clerisso. It's just, eh, I'm a bit stressed out," Tam said, the pitch of his voice fluctuating wildly. Clerisso had this effect on her employees. She was a formidable authoritarian.

"Well, there's deadlines to be met, quotas to be filled etcetera, etcetera. These universes aren't going to create themselves, are they?" She zipped away back to her workstation, leaving a trail of pale purple light behind her.

He had an idea. He moved the cursor to the search tab and typed in 'The Universe Factory'. The familiar grey building came into view. Scrolling through the list of options on his computer screen, Tam clicked on *Edit item* and a text box appeared. If he was struggling with his work in this universe, then why not create an alternate universe where another version of himself didn't have this stress? Knowing somewhere out there, across the dimensions, across time, he could be sitting at his desk, chilling without a care in the universe doing some menial task soothed his soul. Tam wasn't allowed to edit anything except Earth, so he had to be quick. Even from across the room could see Clerisso's beady little eyes glancing up at him every so often. If she caught him doing this he would be out on his arse. Shipped back to Earth with his memory wiped. *Maybe that wouldn't be such a bad thing …*

Tam typed "automate parallel universe creation" and leaned back in his chair. He looked up at Clerisso. She had conjured up a 3D image of a sun and suspended it in the air. She waved her hands and the warm, orange colour of its surface faded to an icy blue.

He leaned forward quickly and hit the *ENTER* key.

Everything on Tam's screen disappeared. He turned to look at Clerisso. She was looking right at him. A pop-up message announced its arrival on the screen with an ominous sound like when a baddie appears in a kid's film. It read: *A fatal error has occurred. Universe production now in overdrive.*

Clerisso landed on Tam's right shoulder. "WHAT THE FUCK DID YOU JUST DO, TAM?!"

"I – I – I – I just thought," Tam stuttered. He turned to his left to look at Frigo. Frigo was staring straight ahead, looking out the window. He turned to Tam.

"Maaaaaaaate," Frigo whispered, barely audible. Tam turned his gaze to the window as well. The black hole around which the Universe Factory orbited was spewing light forth from its centre. The light came out in beams, no thicker than spaghetti, tearing holes in the very fabric of space itself. From the staff room, Tam heard the meal fabricator laughing.

"I'll bet any money that wis fucking daft arse Tam?"

"What's happening? Surely I didn't do that?" Tam said, looking at Clerisso then Frigo.

"Those beams of light are parallel universes leaking into this one. You've fucked it big time, mate," Frigo said.

The strands of light ripped through the Universe Factory. Two of them ripped through Tam's computer monitor. More pop-ups appeared. Clerisso darted around trying to avoid them but it was futile, she was skewered by four of the beams at the same time and more light spilled out of her mouth.

"Get in," Frigo said, enveloping Tam, absorbing him into his body. In an instant, the blinding light was replaced by absolute darkness. The dark smothered Tam with its embrace and he allowed it to take him.

When Tam woke up he was lying on the floor of the office. Several figures came into view as he opened his eyes. Something buzzed around his ears. He raised a hand to bat it away.

"Tam, I swear to fuck," the voice, unmistakably, belonged to Clerisso. She was now less than in inch from his face and the cool breeze from the beat of her wings tickled his nose. "You fall asleep on the job again and you'll be on the first flight back to that fucking shithole you call a planet. You understand?" She fluttered back over to her miniature sun, casting a glance back at Tam and muttering, "Daft cunt."

"Am sorry. Am so sorry," Tam said, climbing back into his seat. Everyone else in the office returned to their desks like nothing had happened. Like the universe hadn't just been torn apart because of his mistake. He turned to look at Frigo. He wondered what the fuck was happening.

"Wit happened there? How is everybody still alive?" Tam asked.

"We've entered that universe I made this morning. I made it so me and you weren't in it, just in case you fucked up. And would you look at that? My decision has been vindicated. Don't try anything like that again, mate, eh?"

"Did you manage to bring anyone else?"

"No, just us. Everyone and everything else in our original universe has been destroyed. It's just a big white vacuum now."

"Fuck," Tam was shaking.

He picked up his coffee and drank it one long gulp. It was freezing cold now, but Tam didn't care. He went through to the staffroom and slumped down into a chair. He thought about handing in his notice. He would have his memory wiped and be sent back to Earth with a new identity. No one there was real though, he realised; they were all just copies. Tam could feel himself going into full-on meltdown mode. He looked over at the meal fabricator.

"Awrite, Tam? Skiving again are we?" the machine asked.

"Just having a wee existential crisis, mate," Tam replied.

"Here," the meal fabricator made a bowl of polyps appear for Tam. "Get these doon ye."

Tam took one look at the glistening, green globules in the bowl and was sick down himself. Back to Earth it was.

OH, 2016

Over in the USA, a vote has been held and a decision made in November 2016 that could change the course of history.

Unfortunately, we go to print just before the outcome of that vote has been reached and we can't *quite* see into the future.

Luckily for you we've got a very high-tech guide on how we continue from here, to cover all eventualities, and a list of our favourite books from 2016.

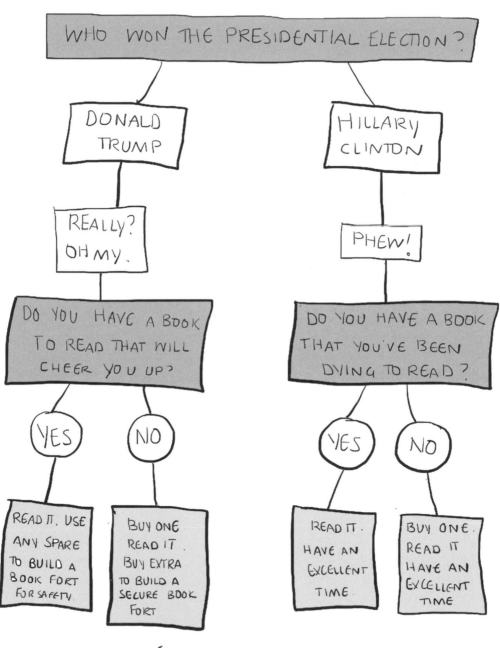

(THANK GOD FOR BOOKS.)

FICTION

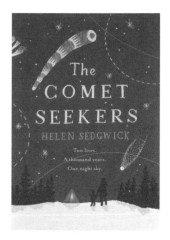

THE COMET SEEKERS by Helen Sedgwick (Harvill Secker)

A lifetime feels a long time, but it's barely a blink of an eye to a comet. Sedgwick encompasses a thousand years in a few hundred pages in a story where the sky is home, adventure, family and a new start.

FEN by Daisy Johnson (Jonathan Cape)

Fen is on one hand quite normal - couples, sex, pubs and marriage frame this short story collection. But within that Johnson weaves tales of magic and darkness and draws you in hook, line and sinker.

HIS BLOODY PROJECT by Graeme Macrae Burnet (Contraband)

It may have snuck out in 2015, but this book made a splash in 2016 by being the surprise guest on the Man Booker shortlist. A brutal triple murder in a remote crofting community in 1869 leads to the arrest of a young man. We know he's guilty – we just need to know why.

THE GIRLS by Emma Cline (Chatto & Windus)

Based on the cult of young women that surrounded Charles Manson, *The Girls* takes a well known story and pushes the horror to the background. All the gruesome details are just an added detail to a book with the girls at the heart.

THE BRILLIANT & FOREVER by Kevin MacNeil (Polygon)

A book where you follow three best friends, where one is an alpaca, is always one to recommend. The annual Brilliant & Forever festival leaves participants facing either glory or infamy. Thirteen performers have a story to tell – who will be chosen?

THE GOOD IMMIGRANT edited by Nikesh Shukla (Unbound)
The Good Immigrant is the most important book of 2016. It's as simple as that. Bringing together 21 exciting black, Asian and minority ethnic voices emerging in Britain today, it explores what it means to be 'other' in a country that doesn't seem to want you.

WHERE AM I NOW? by Mara Wilson (Penguin Books)
You may recognise Mara as Matilda, or the cute little girl in Mrs Doubtfire. But she disappeared from the public eye for many years, and in this collection of essays she travels through her personal life, not being "cute" enough to keep making it in Hollywood, and her shift from childhood fame to more comfortable obscurity. Witty and candid (which is no surprise if you follow her on Twitter), it's a great collection.

THE VIEW FROM THE CHEAP SEATS by Neil Gaiman (Headline)
From speeches to pieces on his friends and peers, career advice to his work in comics and memory of his first Batman, Neil Gaiman leaves no stone unturned in his fascinating non-fiction collection including decades of writing about... well, pretty much everything.

BRUCE SPRINGSTEEN by Born To Run (Simon and Schuster)
The Boss brings the honesty, humour and originality of his songs to the pages that detail his life. From growing up in New Jersey to performing at 2009's Super Bowl halftime show, it's a life you want to read about, from the man himself.

THE MIGHTY WOMEN OF SCIENCE by Clare Forrest, Fiona Gordon (BHP Comics)

From A for Astronaut (Valentina Tereshkova, the first woman in space) to Z for Zoologist (the award winning Biruté Gladikas), The Mighty Women of Science A-Z is a vibrant crash course in vital women in science that history seems to have forgotten over time, bursting with colour and time-travelling adventures. Jump in a time machine and be fascinated.

ALPHA by Bessora, Barroux (Barrington Stoke)

Translated from French, this follows Alpha as he sets off from his home in Côte d'Ivoire for Paris, hoping to find his family, and a new place to call home. This graphic novel is emblematic of the refugee crisis the world currently faces – he's one of millions on the move, frustrated, endangered and exploited on a journey that spans years. An important and timely read that illuminates the plight of thousands, millions, who are just seeking a better life.

THE TROUBLE WITH WOMEN by Jacky Fleming (Square Peg)

"*The Trouble With Women* does for girls what *1066 and All That* did for boys: it reminds us of what we were taught about women in history lessons at school, which is to say, not a lot." On top of learning about great women who were missed off the school curriculum, it's loaded with spoonfuls upon spoonfuls of wit and sarcasm. You'll learn a lot and you'll laugh a lot.

SONNET 404

SONNET 404

CARA L MCKEE

The lifestyle you dreamed of cannot be found.
The kids will complain and the cat will die.
Perhaps it's just temporarily down;
perhaps your fat fingers have failed to type.
Or maybe happiness has been removed:
your country idyll retaken, renamed.
Please check if your typing can be improved,
return to your home page and try again.
You could go back and try another path,
or search for a new way to live your dream.
Your imagined lifestyle will not come back;
the laughter at sunset remains unseen.
The kids will always whine from time to time,
and to the cat we'll raise a glass of wine.

THE ERRONEOUS CALCULUS OF COMPASSION

THE ERRONEOUS CALCULUS OF COMPASSION

IAN MCKENZIE

1.015 million people arrived from the sea in Western Europe as of 31st July 2016. That's 5075 people washed up per day, since January 1st, far from high and dry. 1 guilt-assuaging leaflet stuck with 1 magnet from Turkey on a Beko 320S fridge door offering 31 gifts across 2 web pages. If I'm one of the 45% I will look at these web pages for more than 15 seconds. A shelter for a family from this website costs £14. The average Middle Eastern family is 5 persons. This will cost £2,842,000 to provide 203,000 shelters. £50 provides fresh water for 50 people, I'll need 203,000 sets of that at £50 per set. Each family can have an allotment at £24. This will cost £4,872,000. Veg is not enough to ensure the health of all these persons so £6 buys a health check (£6,090,000). 52% of these people will be children. A classroom for 30 costs £1500. 33,833 class-rooms will be required, costing £50,750,000. This will be an event of more than 6 hours duration, so according to the one and only Health and Safety *Purple Book*, this sounds like a major campsite event with a stipulation for 24,010 WC's and urinals. Fortunately, the website can provide a toilet for £20. This will cost £480,200. In conclusion, £66,049,200 will seem to address the needs of 1.015 million displaced persons. The UK has revenues totalling the equivalent of 939,540,000,000 USD. Attempts to cost and quantify exactly the missing compassion and willingness from Western Europe have proved erroneous. Without this factor the resources described herein are useless unless matched by 'x' quantity of willingness and compassion.

A LIST

BETH COCHRANE

The water spreads across the floor, foam-topped waves waltzing across the ocean surface. I twist the mop into a corner, grinding it against the floor and kitchen cabinet.

I make a list every morning. 'Things To Do'. 'Things' to get through. Important things.

The bathroom's been cleaned and the kitchen is well under way. I've scrubbed and buffed and polished each and every surface and ticked off each task as I go. Soon there will be nothing left on the list and the paper will be lines and scratches; a mottled spider web tracing a map back through time.

But then I'll add more 'Things' and in that way there are always 'Things To Do'. 'Mop Floor', for example. Under subsection: 'Clean Kitchen'.

The radio's on and I pretend I know the words. It would be nice to know something solid, something happening right now that I can follow with a sure foot. Something that others know as fact and truth and can't be, objectively, otherwise. Lyrics, for example, that others could be singing along to beside me, singing the same words in the same seconds all together but unaware of the distant choir accompanying us. So I stumble through some lines, imagining the foregone family I'd never meet. The mouths making the same shapes as my own in that very moment, but soon my imagination closes in on itself as I open my ears and hear the sound of my voice and I grind my teeth together.

I cut my chorus short with a snort of derision and a decision not to embarrass myself in front of myself.

I don't know a thing about music.

Maybe I'll write: 'Listen to More Music' on my 'Things To Do' list:

No. 12. Google: 'Good Music'

Or maybe

No. 12. Google: 'Music Good People Listen To'

People like people who have 'good taste', right?

She always said taste was the most important thing in a person. Maybe I'll move No.12. up on my list, to No.3. or No.4. or maybe right after 'Reply: Parents', which doesn't really seem like such a priority. Maybe I'll buy a record player and some vinyl and maybe you'll be interested and impressed or wonder who has introduced me to this new world.

I break from mopping the floor, dunk the mop into the bucket and it falls back and smacks off the worktop with a dulcet thwack, a bird swooping into a pane of glass and startling the people inside.

Water splashes over the rim of the bucket and it soaks my socks, sending a current of fevered chill through the bones of me. Chill? That water was warm when I filled the bucket and poured in the bleach.

Damn, my socks. I can take them off later.

But I don't like the feel of the wet material against my skin, like having cotton wool in your mouth and rubbing, dragging, along your teeth.

I bend to peel them off and why the fuck not? They've joined the mop in the bucket. Fuck the socks. Socks can dry. They make a pleasing splash as they hit the water, sodden weight pulling them under the surface for a moment but bobbing, eventually, on the buoyant, chemically induced liquid.

The water is under my feet. I feel it seep in between my toes and the soap squelches under my weight. It makes funny little noises; how I imagine tortoises speak to one another, maybe.

I turn the radio up and let it leak into my ears, but 'Music' is still not the first task on my 'Things To Do' list, so it washes over me rather than saturating my memory.

We were in the shower once, water under my feet and running through your hair. Eyes were open and seeing and not understanding that we stood in a world that belongs to other people too. Soap got in my eyes and we lost the moment but it was fine because we laughed and now that memory is safe in my mind, guarded within a hard frost and winter is not thawing anytime soon.

I've let myself take the bait and fall into the trap of unrepentant self-pity from which my 'Things To Do' list stems and keep stagnant.

(Work-In-Progress) – A More Sensible List:

1. Don't fall for that girl who just wants to pass the time with you, when you want to stay up with her all night walking, talking, through the lakes and mountains until we reach the sea and sit by the shore and cliff faces and watch dark swells of water keep pace with our breath.
2. Don't let her ferment in your mind at every waking and unwaking moment like a seed that's fed and watered and grows from sapling to oak within the space of a trite instant.

But I did both those things.

And here you are: my mistake then and my mistake now.

Bubbling in the peripheries no longer, now carving tunnel vision into my eyes and chiseling my pupils so they see only so wide.

With wet feet and chilled blood I decide I want to change things, set fire to the wheels and hurry them into motion.

I take up my mop and push it into new corners of the kitchen. There are some shreds of grated cheddar under the fridge that the hoover has missed. Fuck it, they're somewhere deep within the tendrils of my mop now.

I have a plan.

I'll follow what you said. I'll be sensible and calm and not do anything rash, say anything rash. I'll quietly spend my time breathing until the time is up and words are sent between us again. But then:

1. On your terms, I will build A Bridge. Build it to the specifications I know you would like most. Tailor the plan to you: your 'tastes', your wants. Forget about me, I can change.

The mop skids across the floor a little faster, bursting bubbles with a satisfying pop and lathering a smooth white foam across the tiles.

Soon the whole floor will be white, if I mop long enough and well enough. With the slop of fresh water on the floor, a sock appears on the tiles, lying soggy and limp. It used to be warm and cosy and shield my feet from icy surfaces, but now it's a heap of water-clogged cloth, bedraggled and useless. I drag it here and there across the floor; watch the water flood the brief path it makes through the flood.

2. You'll say yes to the terms, because I built them around you and I know you better than anyone. This may take time, but I'll (we'll) get what I (we) want.

The mop isn't really cleaning anymore. It's just making things wet. It's Sunday and Sunday is cleaning day so I suppose I need to keep going regardless.

I pause my mopping, just for a moment. I bite down on the soft nail of my forefinger, gently ripping the barely white tip and it pulls down a little further, into the nail bed where's it's red and raw and stinging out in the open air. It's down as far as it can be but I don't want to go back to the water and the mop and the floor for a little while longer. I examine each of nail in turn, left hand to right hand, and I see no more left to chew so I grab the skin at the edges. I clutch it in between my teeth and pull a nice, long slice free and spit it out onto the dry floor behind me.

I'll have to sweep that up before I keep mopping.

Another thick slither of skin bitten and spat and the pile grows behind me but I'm running out of flesh around my nails, so I take the mop by the handle once more and swirl, swirl, swirl.

The words you left me with were too kind. Talks of different things and different places – but not different people, it wasn't that, you promised – but maybe that's the problem.

The words didn't leave scars; no proof you'd really tied your shoelaces and fiddled with the lock on my front door for the last time.

But now I have the outlines of a plan.

1. Clean Bathroom
2. Clean Kitchen
3. Fix Us:
    a. Work out, and isolate, the Main Problem
    b. Work out, and carry out, what she would do if positions were switched
    c. Come up with Plan
    d. How to deliver Plan? (d.01: Place/Method of Communication d.02: Time d.03: Manner)
    e. Sort 'issues' with Plan; find solutions ahead of time (don't let her be the 'reasonable' one: be informed, be logical.)
4. Learn what Good Music is & listen to it

Simple steps and it will All Work Out. I dance with the mop. I shove its sodden weight hard against the kitchen units, grinding my teeth down and slamming its saturated fabric into table legs, chair legs, corners and edges, and let my hopes rocket and my future set itself in stone.

I pick up the mop bucket and throw the remaining dirty dregs onto the kitchen floor. The other sock joins its partner awash on the tiles.

The kitchen is one huge puddle now and I jump into the deepest of the miniature floods. Splashing the cabinets and worktops and my own body with the waves of an unseen ocean. I stomp and stamp and thud the heels of my feet hard into the tiles.

Everything is going to be fine. I just have to follow my 'Things To Do' list: simple, effective.

I can even tick things off I as go.

There's no pattern in the water now, but it lies heavy on the floor and the edges of the puddles are starting to dry. Too much cleaning product in the water: it's left behind a weak crust on the tiles, hardening over the surface in veins of white and marrow.

Photo by Leif Laaksonen

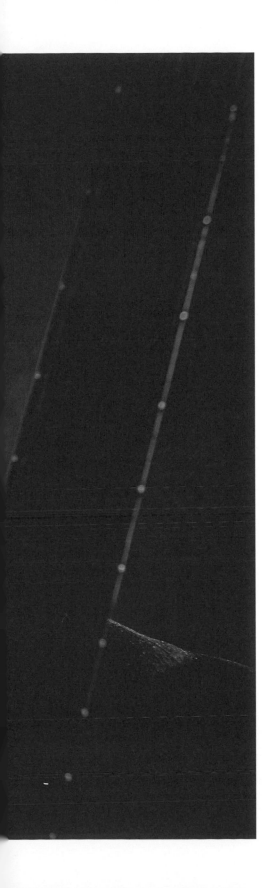

WILKO JOHNSON

Wilko Johnson has never been a man with a plan. His whole approach to life has been to just see where things took him, and roll with it. We've all probably tried it once in a while, but few of us have ended up travelling the world in bands, or starred in things like that little known TV show, *Game of Thrones*, just by rolling with the times.

From the humble beginnings in his home of Canvey Island, Wilko and the inimitable Lee Brilleaux and John B. Sparks formed Dr. Feelgood and became a staple of the pub rock scene in London through the 1970s. With belters 'She Does It Right' and 'Roxette' in their repertoire, it was all going well until tensions arose, and Wilko left, or was booted out, depending on who you ask. He never went back to the drawing board, instead going full steam ahead: he played with a few more bands, including The Blockheads with Ian Dury, but it was The Wilko Johnson Band that stuck, and kept him travelling the world with his guitar in tow for the last several decades.

Each twist has been an unexpected adventure for Wilko, and that's why, come January 2013, when he was told that he had terminal pancreatic cancer and just ten months to live, he embraced the news in a way that fit with his past seven decades.

Today is, quite obviously, more than ten months later than when the news was broken, and now Wilko has written a book – *Don't You Leave Me Here* – that takes you through his childhood, life spent with wife Irene, the iconic rise and fall of Dr Feelgood, and that last year of his life… but a few years on.

"I hadn't written a book before. I didn't have any method, so I just launched into it haphazardly. Started thinking 'Ayyy, man, I'm a writer!', you know?" laughs Wilko. "I'd open the ol' laptop, tap away pretty good. I found after I got into it, I started getting into some sad stuff, like when my wife died, and aw, man…

"Normally when we remember things, look back on them, we remember them in bits and pieces, we just remember one scene or one day or event or something like that. When you need to write a book, of course you've got to remember whole periods in a sequence, and you get to the sad bits and, aw, man, it all comes back on me as if it was yesterday. Oh dear, I was so upset and I couldn't write. I just opened the laptop and I'm just sitting there crying there and upset like a complete wimp.

"Anyway, I kind of pull myself together and carried on. What the result was – whether it's good or bad – I do not know."

I'VE LIVED MY WHOLE LIFE DRIFTING INTO THINGS ACCIDENTALLY.

The book is indeed a good result and one that takes you down the streets of Canvey Island, around the pubs of London, the stages and studios of the world. With a life so full of stories to tell, it's unsurprising that as he revisited his life, many stories that were long lost in the back of his memory started coming to life.

When Dr. Feelgood split up, Wilko didn't look back and instead focused on what music would come next. In fact, when he came to write the book, the band were a mere blip on the radar originally. "When that happened all those years ago I remember, at the time, it was a blow to me," he admits, "but I resolved to walk away from it and never look badly on it. I just wanted to remember Dr. Feelgood as a great thing and I've never in my mind or otherwise indulged in recriminations or anything. So, I just kind of skimmed over it. I just said, 'Well, we had an argument and broke up.'

"Lemmy [Kilmister, Motörhead] told me that his theory was speed freaks and drunks could never get on well together and that's what I said. The publishers said, 'You can't just say that! You've got to explain a bit more.'

"I tried to remember what happened at that moment in time and as I remembered more and more, I thought, those bastards! They did me wrong! They lied about me and they blamed me for that break up and it wasn't me, man, it was them. And I got quite angry – I thought blimey, man, I was right and they were wrong. They did me wrong and I wasn't to blame for Dr. Feelgood breaking up, it was them. Right? And, well, that's it. I really, really never looked on it or relived it or anything up until that moment actually trying to write about it."

Many stories like that appear in his autobiography that he admits he didn't really think too much about the time, instead too busy just rocking and rolling wherever the music took him.

"I've lived my whole life drifting into things accidentally," he reflects. "I've never had ambitions or aims, I just let things happen, and Dr. Feelgood was no different. I loved that rhythm and blues music and I just wanted to play, and that's what we did, without any kind of ambition. I just got swept along

with it. When we started that band, as I say, it was just the sheer pleasure of playing music – I didn't realise that was going to be my life.

"I always thought that Dr. Feelgood was going to be my band, you know? I was never going to go on and do anything else," he notes, considering whether there was even an alternative to music once he'd had that first taste. "It's a pretty good life! It's a very good life. I just wanted to continue and so I did, as ever, keep drifting along and drifting along and that's how my career has been – consisting of ups and downs. Now I'm an old man and I look back and think, 'Yeah, that was a pretty good thing to do.' And I'll probably be doing it until I drop."

WELL, THIS IS ANOTHER ADVENTURE.

Photo by Leif Laaksonen

Wilko means it. When he was living what doctors had deemed his last year on Earth, he didn't seek out a cure or waste a second trying to buy more time. He lived exactly as he wanted to.

"That year was one of the most extraordinary years of my life, actually," he beams, adding "when I was dying of cancer. I think everybody must imagine to themselves sometimes, well, what would I feel if one day the doctor said to me I'm gonna die? We imagine all sorts of things.

"When that happened to me, I was sitting there looking across the desk at the doctor and he's saying those words to me: 'You've got cancer.' And I was absolutely calm, not a tremor. I said 'Okay.'

"They told me that they thought I had just a few months to live, and I thought, 'Well this is another adventure,'" he laughs. "What can you do? Start screaming and crying and fall on the floor? No. You think – wow. This is another one. Walking out of the hospital – it was a beautiful winter's day, looking up at the trees against the sky – aw, man, it looked so beautiful and suddenly I felt this rush. I felt ecstatic. Man, I'm alive. I'm alive! It was just so intense, and I just hadn't felt like that for years. You're looking around and thinking how beautiful everything looks – oh wow! – and so the year went on.

"As I say, it was the most extraordinary year. Lots of strange things happened. At the end of that year, when the time had come that they

reckoned I was going to die at ten months and I was already into my eleventh – Roger Daltrey [of The Who] popped up and said let's make an album together," chuckles Wilko. "I'm thinking maaan, ain't life weird? Here I am, my life is ending, and I can't complain, I've just had a fantastic life and here I am ending up making an album with Roger Daltrey.

"When we were making that album I didn't think I was going to live to see it released. In fact, I did live to see it released, and it was the most successful album I've ever done. It got a Gold Disc. I remember thinking, this is crazy man – I've got a bestselling album, a Gold Disc, and now I'm gonna die.

"But NO! There was another surprise in store."

I SHOULD'VE BEEN IN MY GRAVE TWO YEARS AGO.

The surprise was a fated meeting with Charlie Chan, a surgeon who also did music photography – he recommended Wilko get a second opinion and so he came to meet Emmanuel Huguet, the surgeon who would save his life. "These doctors found me and told me they thought they could cure me," he says simply. "And they did. And that was weird upon weird. It was always strange."

While facing death, he was euphoric, full of life by his own account. He's a

couple of years into a future he didn't think he'd have, and still finds it odd to reconcile this latest twist in his adventure. "Today, I'm looking out my window. It's a beautiful day here and, again, looking at the trees against the sky." He bursts out laughing – again. It's hard not to be swept along in his positivity. "When I got the cancer diagnosis, what did I do? I thought, well: I've got ten months left to live, I just want to enjoy it, make the most of these ten months. I didn't go looking for second opinions or miracle cures, I thought I'm going to go ahead, carry on playing.

"This tumour was growing the whole time. It got so big it looked liked I was pregnant. This tumour was the size of a melon in my stomach. I used to stand on the stage and my guitar used to rock on this tumour. You could never get away from it.

"This whole thing started, me sitting across a table from a doctor and the doctor telling me, 'You're going to die.' A year later I'm sitting again across the table from a doctor and the doctor is telling me he thinks he can cure me. I've spent more than a year convinced

I'm dying and there's nothing that can be done and then there was this man, this supernatural guy, telling me that he thought they could do it. And so they did.

"Man, it knocks it out of you. They opened me up and took half of my gut away and as well as this tumour that weighed three and a quarter kilos. They took that out of me, they took away my pancreas and my spleen, they took away half of my stomach, and stitched me up, and then I'm lying on my back weak as a kitten for months recovering in the hospital and at home.

"And here I am.

"It's weird to say – here I am! If I try and talk about it now, I think here I am, looking out the window at them trees, talking to somebody about it and then thinking 'Man, I should've been in my grave two years ago,' and that's very, very hard to comprehend. Here I am."

Wilko may never have been a man with a plan, but here he is on the latest stop of one hell of an adventure.

Don't You Leave Me Here by Wilko Johnson is out now. Published by Little, Brown, £18.99.

WHY DO WE PUT A HAT ON ROCKY THE SQUIRREL

WHY DO WE PUT A HAT ON ROCKY THE SQUIRREL?

KATERINA SIDOROVA

Cat, you tumble down the street
As if it were your bed.
I think such luck is a treat,
Like feeding without being fed.

You're just a pawn in the hands
Of fate, as stones are, and people!
You follow your instinct and glands;
What you feel you feel -- it's simple.

Because you are like that you are happy;
You're all the nothing you see.
I look at myself -- it's not me.
I know myself -- I'm not I.

Fernando Pessoa

One thing to begin with. Humans are never reflecting on animal life, they are constantly reflecting on their own. What do they want from an animal when they speak about it, or, more importantly, when they speak for it?

I am probably eight or nine years old, sitting at home and watching *The Rocky & Bullwinkle Show*, an American animated television series from the mid-sixties. The main character is Rocky the squirrel, a flying squirrel to be more precise. He is optimistic, energetic and humorous.

It is surprising how easily I can relate to Rocky. I like him a lot. I do not realise that I am looking at an animal, I am looking at a character. Still, I see Rocky precisely as a squirrel, not as a human boy and this very squirrel is very likely to become a great friend of mine.

The true tragedy of incompatibility occurred to me only years later. Never ever would I be able to speak to any representative of the Flying Squirrel species, because they have no perception of language. Never will we be friends, because squirrels do not know of friendship. Never will Rocky laugh at my jokes, as it is not aware of what humour is.

What is a squirrel busy with instead?

Let's first see how it looks:

A female Siberian flying squirrel weighs about 150 grams, the males being slightly smaller on average. The body is 13–20 cm long, with a 9–14 cm long flattened tail. The eyes are large and strikingly black. The coat is gray all over, the abdomen being slightly lighter than the back, with a black stripe between the neck and the forelimb. A distinctive feature of flying squirrels is the furry glide membrane or patagium, a flap of skin that stretches between the front and rear legs. By spreading this membrane the flying squirrel may glide from tree to tree across distances of over a hundred meters, and have been known to record a glide ratio of 3.31, but is normally 1-1.5.[1]

Now the squirrel's habits:

Its diet consists of leaves, seeds, cones, buds, sprouts, nuts, berries and occasionally bird eggs and nestlings. When alder and birch catkins are plentiful, the squirrel may store them for the winter in old woodpecker holes or similar nooks. The squirrels are preyed upon by martens, owls, and cats. They mate early in the spring. After a gestation period of five weeks, the female gives birth to a litter of usually two or three young, each weighing about 5 grams. They preferentially build their nest in holes made by woodpeckers, but they may also nest in birdhouses if the size of the entrance is appropriate. The nest consists of a pile of soft materials (preferably soft beard lichen) into which the squirrel burrows. They can live up to about five years.

They favour old forests with a mix of conifers and deciduous trees. They are mostly nocturnal, being most active late in the evening, although females with young may also feed during the day. They do not hibernate, but in the winter they may sometimes sleep continuously for several days. As shy and nocturnal animals, they are seldom seen. The most common

---

1   Asari, Y; Yanagawa, H.; Oshida, T. (2007). "Gliding ability of the Siberian flying squirrel Pteromys volans orii". Mammal Study 32(4): Retrieved 2009-07-14, p. 324

sign of their presence is their droppings, which resemble orange-yellow rice grains and are often found beneath or on top of their nest.[2]

Not being able to communicate to a squirrel verbally, we decided to name it, to describe it, characterise it. And we chose a great word for it – an animal.

"The animal, what a word! The animal is a word, it is an appellation that men have instituted, a name they have given themselves the right and the authority to give to another living creature," wrote Jacques Derrida.

We, humans, came up with this word. We named all the animals too. By naming them, categorising, we opposed ourselves to animals. The gap created between the two now has lead to a lack of understanding, which then lead to us romanticising the very idea of being an animal. This action is followed by taking an image of an animal, that we chose for specific reasons which have emotional value to us. On that image we project the assumption that by not being granted with consciousness, an animal is an eternally happy being, as it knows not the distinction between happiness and sorrow.

We do not take any middle ground, we choose to oppose. We see no in-between. (But maybe we can try? Deleuze and his becoming-animal come to my mind already, but let's save them for a little later.)

The fact that the lack of some objects or qualities of desire becomes a positive thing is in itself problematic. One finds it normal to envy someone else's riches. But in the case of an animal we are jealous of the poor. We are jealous of those who lack what we have. We assume animals to lack intelligence and therefore are free from moral judgments, free from fears and expectations that we, humans cannot escape from. M. Heidegger proposes three theses, which are:

1. The stone is without the world.
2. The animal is poor with the world.
3. Man is world-forming.

J. Derrida explains that these three theses prepare the reader to the question "What is the world?" I will not try to get anywhere near this question, instead choosing to stick to "How do any of these entities relate to what is called the world?" – a slightly simpler thing to wonder about.

Here I, after reading Derrida, who read Heidegger, will attempt to explain the word "poverty". In this case it does not specifically mean the lack or a smaller quantity of possessing something, but more a different manner of accessing that

---

2   Idem, p. 326

special something. Let us call that something "the world", or very roughly, the sum of all the possible entities.

> It is not that the animal has a lesser relationship, a more limited access to entities, it has an *other* relationship [...] The animal can have a world because it has access to entities, but it is deprived of a world because it does not have access to entities as such and in their Being. The worker bee, says Heidegger, knows the flower, its colour and its scent, but it does not know the flower's stamen as a stamen, it does not know the roots, the number of stamens, etc. The lizard, whose time on the rock, in the sun, Heidegger describes laboriously and at length, does not relate to the rock and the sun as such, as that with regard to which, precisely, one can put questions and give replies. And yet, however little we can identify with the lizard, we know that it has a relationship with the sun—and with the stone, which itself has none, neither with the sun nor with the lizard.[3]

The lizard wouldn't call a rock a rock, the bee wouldn't name a plant a plant, as they cannot access these definitions, as they cannot access language. Heidegger, again, says:

> "The leap from the animal that lives to man that speaks is as great, if not greater, than that from the lifeless stone to the living being." This inability to name is not primarily or simply linguistic; it derives from the properly phenomenological impossibility of speaking the phenomenon whose phenomenology as such, or whose very as such, does not appear to the animal and does not unveil the Being of the entity. [...] Here the erasure of the name would signify the non-access to the entity as such."[4]

And one most important quote: "It is clear that the animal can be after a prey, it can calculate, hesitate, follow or try out a track, but it cannot properly question."[5] No questions – no replies. That is it. We define things, we seek for answers in the outside world, already knowing that they can only come within us. Our scream of despair is nothing against the silent acceptance of an animal.

Now what we have is a human being, who came up with such a definition, who is painfully aware of it. I imagine he says to himself "I named things and I

---

3   Derrida, J. Of Spirit: Heidegger and the Question, trans. Geoffrey Bennington & Rachel Bowlby (Chicago & London: University of Chicago Press, 1989.

4   Idem

5   Idem

described their qualities. I look at these things and I do know when they expire. The animal next to me has no such knowledge and is therefore free from the weight that comes with it. There my jealousy arises. I envy the one who does not know what envy is. In a pouring rain I seek for my umbrella and I envy those who will not know of the comfort it brings."

Is a squirrel happy? He will not tell us. He will never speak to us. Never will he explain to us what life and its things are all about. Does he know? He will not tell us that either. And for that we are jealous.

Now look at what we have done to Rocky the flying squirrel. We put an aviator hat on his head, we let him ride in a car. Most importantly, we gave him an ability to speak and to understand speech. We grant him with the knowledge of English language and all the evaluative categories that come with it. Now Rocky has a name that he will reply to. He has emotions and insecurities. He worries about his future, about his life being stable. He is ambitious too, he wants to find his life's calling. If worse comes to worst he will even want to try make sense out of his own existence. He is now fully humanised, loaded with our never ending questioning. He will pay us back.

But then, *The Rocky & Bullwinkle Show* ends, the titles run, and yet again all we are left with is observing the "blissful not knowing" animals. We can try to domesticate them; we can teach birds to say human words but we will never understand them and they will never care enough to try and understand us. This will make us sadder; still the bastards would not care, as they don't have the means to.

We will also never stop opposing ourselves to them; no matter how many Hegels, Heideggers, Derridas or Braidottis it will take. Discourses will change, but we are still as romantic, envying the kitty cat's playful naivety that we ourselves granted it with.

We will go back to desperate attempts of antropomorphicising them. More Rockys, Bremen musicians, Toms and Jerrys, SpongeBobs and Sandy the Squirrels will come.

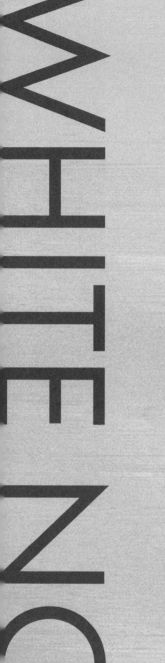

WHITE NOISE

WHITE NOISE

GAVIN INGLIS

The audio had become a grating, vibrating white noise which rattled Gunjan's eardrums and chiselled straight into his brain. The public address system was just visible at the other end of the cellar, black rectangular speakers nestled in shadow, tireless. Had it been hours? Days? When he'd awakened, his watch was missing. Still, he had his jeans, shirt and dastar, a bottle of water and a pot for a toilet. There had been no violence; just this relentless wall of sound.

Somehow, through the cacophony, Gunjan heard a door open, shrieking on rusty hinges. He sat back against the cold wall and stared at the silhouette which entered. If he could discern some tell-tale detail, any clue to the identity of his abductor … but the spotlights had been placed to prevent this, to create a patch of illumination that matched the range of Gunjan's chains.

The figure crossed to the mixing desk and lowered the volume to a social level. Still he felt it there, buzzing like a hornet.

"You've got the wrong person," said Gunjan, with as much composure as he could manage. "I'm not a spy or a terrorist. I'm just a shopkeeper. Please. Why are you doing this?"

The man regarded him for thirty seconds.

"It's a free country," he said. Then he turned the volume back up and left.

Sometime during the next period – perhaps it was hours, perhaps only minutes – Gunjan felt his reason fray a little. Strand by strand, his thoughts unwound. He forced himself to focus on the positive. The manacles were heavy, but he could place his wrists flat or lie down when he felt the pins and needles in his arms. The noise alone could not hurt him.

When the man returned, he seemed to bring coloured echoes of his shape, slightly misaligned like a bad screenprint. By now Gunjan was seeing things at the periphery of his vision; dark little shapes skittering through the light. He knew he was hallucinating. He had been sleep deprived before, but only after the best of parties.

"You're having trouble thinking clearly," his captor said. "I can see it in your eyes. Lack of sleep affects your capacity to concentrate. But did you know it also affects your skin? When you don't get enough sleep, your body releases more cortisol. The stress hormone. That breaks down the collagen that keeps your skin smooth and elastic. It's not just dark circles under the eyes. Eventually, your whole body will become dry and painful. It doesn't matter how much water you drink." A fresh bottle thumped to the floor beside Gunjan.

"Why are you doing this? Are you a racist?" he spat, with more bravado than he felt.

The man gave a short laugh. He walked behind the mixer and adjusted something. What was there? Was it a computer? The noise dropped in pitch a little. Gunjan frowned. He could begin to hear a pattern, some kind of scrambled rhythm. It was a relief to hear it change.

Not for long. At this pitch, the sound hit harder. It was almost recognisable, and yet still beyond him; a collection of frequencies piercing his ears like a pincushion. He huddled on the cold cellar floor. The manacles would only let him plug one ear at a time.

The next time, he didn't even see the door open. He had become obsessed with a feeling that somebody was watching him from behind. His captor seemed to move in strange, sudden bursts of speed.

"I know what you're doing," Gunjan croaked.

"Yes?" The man seemed curious.

"You're softening me up for interrogation. I saw a programme about this technique on TV. You're not letting me sleep so I'll be confused and compliant. Look, you're making a mistake. You have the wrong person. Ask me anything. I'll answer."

"What does Scotland mean to you?"

"… What?"

"What does Scotland mean to you?"

"I …" He stared.

"Mmm-hmm." The man lowered the pitch again and left. For a few moments it was a relief, then the sound struck back, harder again. He could grasp it now. It was music, songs run together and sped up beyond recognition. Shredded voices tore through it, whining melody; bass turned into a pneumatic drill. The shivers started soon after, the tears. In desperation Gunjan threw his toilet pot towards the mixer. The manacles arrested his throw and it dropped short. He had to piss in the empty water bottle.

"You're wondering if it's night or day. It's day. It's always day when I come. I work the night shift. Does that mean anything to you?" The figure leaned in. "I see not. It wasn't even significant enough for you to remember."

The man was close now. Close enough to touch but Gunjan had no strength left. No voice left.

"I'll give you one last clue."

He strolled back to the source and adjusted something, staring at Gunjan. The noise slowed, slowed, blurred and resolved into familiar music. Gunjan lifted his head.

"That's right. You know this. What is it?"

He did know it. It was on his iPod. Something from one of the albums he …

"It's 'Going Home'. By the Royal Scots Dragoon Guards. Based on the Mark Knopfler original, from the soundtrack to *Local Hero*. You recognise it now? And the 'Skye Boat Song'. And 'Caledonia'. And 'Amazing Grace' and 'Charlie Is My Darling'. I know all these songs every bit as well as you because YOU PLAYED THEM FUCKING CONSTANTLY UNDER MY FUCKING BEDROOM WINDOW EVERY DAY FROM YOUR STUPID FUCKING TARTAN TAT SHOP FOR SIX MONTHS. While I was trying to sleep. And when I gave up on the police and the noise wardens and asked you, very, very politely, and almost in tears, to please keep your loudspeakers inside the shop and not point them out into the street, do you remember what you said? 'It's a free country.' Seems ironic now. Eh?"

Gunjan gaped at him. "I am, honestly, sorry. I regret that now. I'll take the speakers in. I won't say anything about this. Please. Don't hurt me."

The man loomed very close. "I'm not going to hurt you. In fact, I'm going to get you some food. I need to find out what you like because I'm going to be bringing you food for another …" He checked his watch. "… five months and twenty-five days."

Gunjan shook his head, and then, finally, he screamed. But the sound of his distress was blotted out by the opening refrain of a familiar, deafening, bagpipe version of 'Donald, Where's Yer Troosers?'

HOW TO WALK QUIETLY

[1] Note: remember to open and close the door as slowly as possible, to avoid slamming it against the wall or back into its frame.

[2] Both are to be avoided at all costs.

[3] It is just too much for you to handle right now.

[4] Note: If this is too tricky to manoeuvre at this time due to alcohol consumption, you may have to accept that it will be a job for the morning and may progress on to the next stage.

HOW TO WALK QUIETLY

KARYN DOUGAN

Your first challenge is the keyhole. Time spent here can be between one and three minutes, following a typical pattern of: three/five attempts to guide the key into the lock, twist, take out, try another key, twist, take out, put first key back in, twist, successfully unlock the door.[1]

Needless to say it is **essential** to remove your heels, especially if you have a wooden floor – an assault course of creaky floorboards lies ahead. Removing heels will reduce noise and decrease chances of you falling on your arse.[2]

Depending on the amount of alcohol you have consumed, you are faced with two options:

1.   Sleep on the sofa
2.   Manoeuvre yourself upstairs to bed

As it's December and the heating broke two months ago, you opt for the riskier option of bed.

Your next challenge: the stairs. Pace is **crucial**. If you feel inclined, crawl on all fours. No one will be watching.

It is inevitable that you may need to throw up in the bathroom. Remember to lift your hair back as you bend over the toilet. You may even be tempted to have a shower whilst there – an attempt to wash away the last few hours. To clean off any particulars common from a One Night Stand. Avoid this.[3]

No lights. You may use your phone to guide you to your side of the bed. Unzip your Little Black Dress slowly.[4]

You may then proceed to ease yourself into your side of the bed. Make sure not to touch him. This will be all he needs to pretend to wake up.

Have your phone on silent so neither of you can hear those incoming texts asking to see you again.

Be careful not to think about what will happen in the morning.

Please remember to cry quietly.

ERROR

BY THOMAS HEITLER

GENTLEMEN OF THE BOARD, WE ARE AT THE FOREFRONT OF ROBOTICS!

I AM PLEASED TO ANOUNCE THE NEXT GENERATION OF ARTIFICIAL PERSONS.

BUILT TO THE HIGHEST STANDARDS, AND TECH INNOVATION,

AT OUR WORLD CLASS FACILTY WE ARE FORGING THE FUTURE!

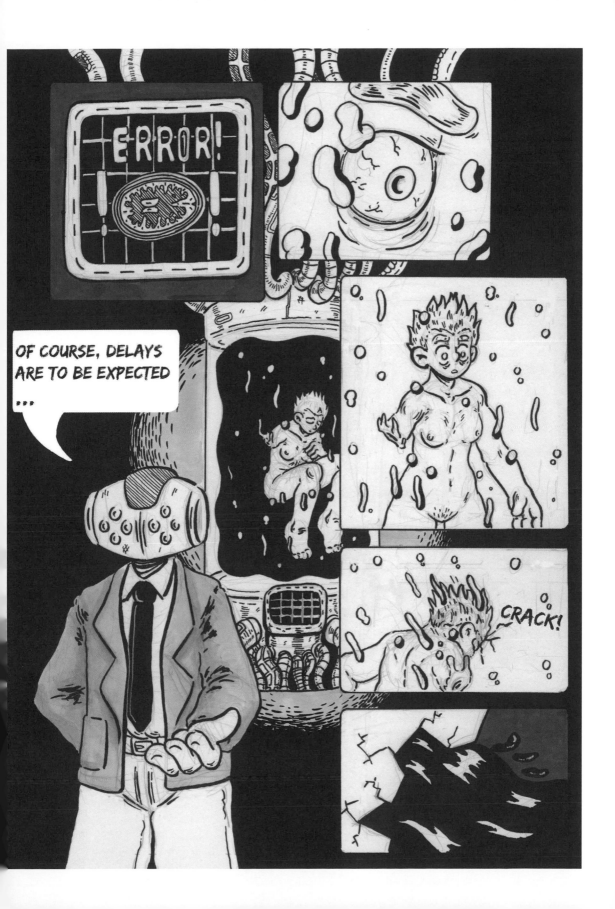

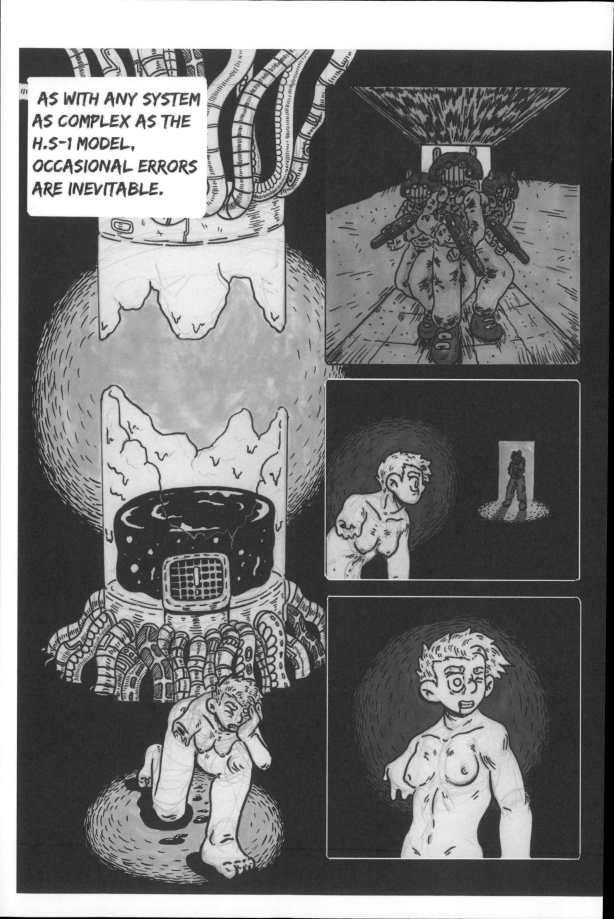

AS WITH ANY SYSTEM AS COMPLEX AS THE H.S-1 MODEL, OCCASIONAL ERRORS ARE INEVITABLE.

THE

PUBLISHING DEAL

THE PUBLISHING DEAL

KEVIN MACNEIL

I made myself into a piece of furniture. The organisers wanted me to be more of a robot, wandering among the talkative guests, moving the drinks tray towards them, perhaps while mouthing, "Red or white?"

But over here a couple of intriguing characters were embarking on an exchange I couldn't pull myself away from, so I decided to stay as still as a standard lamp and let the writers and publishers and civilians come to me for their reds or whites.

I was 25 and struggling through one temporary job after another while working on a humorous novel.

In London, this was. Bloomsbury. A beautiful June evening stretched and shimmered outside.

Inside, a garrulous gathering of authors and publishers, both accomplished and aspiring, chattered at each other, gesticulating with their non-drinkholding hand.

Close to where I stood, an oddball was attempting to engage the attention of a highly polished older man.

The strange little man was wearing an outfit – more an outdoesn'tfit – of red chinos, orange waistcoat, yellow shirt, none of which seemed remotely the right size. His moustache was 1970s, his mullet 1980s, his lobe-stretching ear-rings 1990s. He had a gleam in his eye that was either hungry for experience, ambitious for recognition or outright deranged.

"'Scuse me," he said in an Essex accent, "did I hear you say you're a publisher?"

The older man looked down at him. "Yes," he replied, "I'm Godfrey Big Bloody Publisher." He made to move away, but the eccentric fellow stalled him by thrusting his hand out. "Derek Lee. You want to sign me up, you do."

The distinguished publisher reluctantly shook Derek's hand and with equal disinterest said, "Are you an author?"

Derek withdrew his hand, beaming, and jabbed a thumb towards himself. "Listen, mate. I'm as mad as a dolphin-flavoured cheesecake."

The eminent gentleman winced, and muttered, "Beg your pardon?"

"Bonkers, I am," said Derek. "I make Sylvia Plath look like Mary Berry."

Godfrey Big Bloody Publisher glanced across the room, perhaps at a genuine acquaintance, said, "Ah," and made off in that direction.

"Watch this," said Derek, blocking the older man's escape. He grabbed two glasses, one of each colour, off my tray. "Red wine." He guzzled half a glass of red. "White wine." He knocked back half the glass of white like a shot. "Watch." He poured the remainder of the white wine into the glass of red and mixed them with his finger. "Now." He looked about. I was positioned near the bar, handy for replenishing my drinks tray. A large publisher – perhaps Godfrey's own – had provided a varied bar of harder drinks, and it was tacitly understood that this was exclusively to refresh an elite group of writers and publishers; our trays carried only cheap wine. "Ah yes," said Derek. "Vodka." He picked up a bottle of Finnish vodka and added a splash to his glass of wines. "Ooh, what's that green bottle? Absinthe, I hope." It was. He poured a measure of absinthe into the disgusting mixture. He raised the glass in cheers to Godfrey and said, "Down the hatch." He swallowed the poisonous concoction in one horrendous gulp. Just watching him made my stomach flinch. Godfrey said, "I really don't think that's advisable," but the drink was already gone.

Derek wiped his mouth on a garish yellow, too-long sleeve. "Delicious! I make Dylan Thomas look like the Archbishop of Canterbury. And see this …"

"A mobile phone. Very good," said Godfrey. "But I must go over there and see a friend …"

"Not the phone," said Derek excitedly. "The photos. The photos!"

Godfrey looked, and no doubt felt, a little trapped but his expression changed as he peered at the phone. 'I say, is that …?"

"A picture of me wrestling a shark? Yes it is!" Derek shone with tipsy pride. I tried to steal a look at his phone, but the photo had changed to one of …

"Me doing mixed martial arts against two grizzly bears. And here I am punching a killer whale in the face. I make Ernest Hemingway look like Emily Dickinson, I do."

Godfrey gently shook his head, frowning. "I wish you the best …"

Derek reeled on his feet, taken aback. "But where is it?"

"It?"

"My publishing contract."

Now Godfrey was the one whose face registered astonishment. "Whatever gave you the deluded impression I'd present you with a publishing contract?"

"That's the traditional way," said Derek, sounding wounded. "Be mad. Drink an ocean of booze. Live a life on the edge. That's what writers do."

"My good fellow," said Godfrey, "we are living in more enlightened times. Mental health is no small matter. We have programmes and facilities to help with that. Alcoholism is a life-threatening disease. And as for that macho Hemingway bull …"

"Was that a pun?"

"Do take this seriously, please. I don't much like humour. Humour doesn't win prizes. As I was saying, that macho Hemingway posturing has been thankfully superseded by a greater awareness of gender issues. This is the twenty-first century; we don't expect such shallow behaviour from our authors. How do I know you can even write?"

Derek swallowed, crestfallen. "So – so I'm not getting a publishing contract?"

Godfrey, nearing exasperation, said, "No! Certainly not. My advice to you is – get with the times."

If my hands weren't full I believe I may have reached out and placed a reassuring palm on Derek's shoulder, perhaps passed on some words of advice, one writer to another. But Derek wasn't finished yet. "I *am* a modern writer, though. I have eighty-two thousand Twitter followers."

Godfrey's face perked up and I flinched, overbalancing; I dropped my tray, spilling cheap wine all over his shoes, thereby losing my job. Before I was asked to leave I clearly heard Godfrey inviting Derek to lunch so they could discuss his ideas further.

Outside, under the few twinkling stars London afforded, I tried to appreciate the cool breeze. I looked down from the stars to the streetlights and thought of the constancy that furniture achieves. I considered the life-enhancing things that trees can become, like tables, and I wondered if it was possible to write a great book that would sit in people's lives like a table, clear and useful.

Perhaps other people shall one day dine on my dreams.

I shall first of all become a better piece of the furniture myself.

PROPHECY FALLS

PROPHECY FALLS

JAMIE NORMAN

The fox who longed for grapes, beholds with pain
The tempting clusters were too high to gain

The Fox and the Grapes, Aesop fable

Each night we see you
Wrapped up in the fox,
We watch as its
White peaks rend
Setting to work again
Worrying your china
That fragile painted skin

We count each puncture
Measuring them against (   )
Our own,   bre(   )hing
Air into them(   )
Counting(   )
Fibres and (   ) floss
Strings of ribbon (   )
Tangled under your silk(   )skin
Every night, we tell you
You will always be beautiful

To us, you pay no heed
Twisted in on yourself, round
And again you watch the fox
And the teeth and the holes
And perhaps I think you can hear
The dripping where fluid

Spills through burst welts like pipping
We watch as it moves to your hands
Greedy and rich with the vim of life
Snapping each wishbone finger with
A crack   a crack   a crack

It's how we like to see you
(   ) in magenta, orange, white and red
          (   )deep plumbs and dripping, oiled velvets
                    (   )re fluid than formed
               (   )n the fox
                    (   )below its head
               (   )is caught up in you
Fused in y(   )radecent sprays of colour
(   )
You, the vibrant screaming life
Our empty room is unworthy
Of your ambience, your colour
Blue does not suit you

It   is   vast

The stuffed fox was our
Present, to you small
Ferality, but vivid, alive
Now we hope that it could
Bring some colour, back
To your azure
Your yellowed eyes
Your strangled neck

We hoped that you could meet it.
Why wouldn't you fight   for   us

It would have been better
Than   fading

(   )

REBOOT

REBOOT

NICHOLAS J. PARR

As he stood in front of the gathered crowd and cleared his throat to speak, Thomas recalled his very first memory. One autumn afternoon in the back garden he collected insects amongst the long grass, climbed trees and played fetch with his dog. When his mother called him in for supper he entered the house with great reluctance. At the side of the house he had left the latch on the garden gate up. A gentle breeze swung it open and, of course, the dog escaped. Sniffing at the air, overwhelmed by removed boundaries. The old widowed lady from two doors down found her at the bottom of the driveway and came to their front door, hysterical. He listened from the stairs as she told his mother the news. Before she had finished, he ran down the stairs and pushed past both of them onto the street. Stood witness to the horror he had caused. Glass eyes and head twisted, a jut of bone from a compound fracture, most likely a rib. Fur matted in the blood pooling in the gutter. *I didn't see it,* the old lady cried, *I didn't see it, why was it loose?* she cried and fanned her wrinkled face and soon he began to cry too. He didn't need a punishment for that mistake (prognosis is: *an error of youth*).

He was older now but not by much. Patched stubble and sad sunken eyes unconvincing attempts to validate his age. On the twelfth and penultimate level of a disused parking garage the crowd stood watching him, dressed in office attire with loose ties and creased shirts. Onlookers waiting for the confession. A couple smoked cigarettes. Others conversed in hushed tones. All voyeurs of some terrible but unavoidable occurrence of which they would all suffer eventually. Today it just happened to be young Thomas stood on the soapbox before them, paraded like a leper. Preparing a sermon from the accused and flawed. The shamed boy saw the worn white lines and arrows on the concrete walls and floors around him that now pointed nowhere. He hesitated and took a deep breath, the undue pause causing the crowd to murmur. The priest stood behind his left shoulder, put a firm hand on it, and leaned in to whisper, "Come on now, Thomas. You have come this far."

"I'm scared, Father."

"We are all scared, my son. But you need to confess."

Another deep breath and the boy steadied himself. Somewhere far above a plane soared. On the street below a man sneezed. Thomas imagined him reaching into his top shirt pocket for a handkerchief. These moments, soon to be lost. Oh well.

"I'm here confess to my recent mistakes. Before I list them I want to say I'm sorry." His tortured voice broke and he had paused once more. "I didn't mean to put anyone in any danger."

"Quit stalling, Tommy!" a burly man yelled from the crowd, "Face the music. Go out like a man."

"If you are only here to berate the boy you can leave." The priest's voice both loud and calm, his hand still resting firmly on the boy's shoulder. "Please. Keep going, Thomas."

"I stole a car last year and took it for a ride. It was close to here, actually. You are all older and most of you can drive. I wanted to learn."

"You learnt pretty damn quick," came from within the listening crowd.

"I did. I enjoyed it. I kept driving and driving around the city until the car ran out of petrol, then I abandoned the car and came home."

"He doesn't sound sorry!" A flash of anger from the audience.

"I *am* sorry."

"It's easy to say that now."

"Enough!" The priest stood in front of Thomas and held one arm up.

"I know I was lucky I wasn't caught and I now know the severity of my actions. I was young."

"You still are, Thomas. It was an unprecedented danger and it could have put us in a compromising position. It was an error of youth, an error in judgement. But since the incident you have been respectful and grown in maturity. You responded well."

The wind picked up and howled through the levels of the garage, its structure hollow and meaningless. If the wind could speak would it tell him to run? To attempt life somewhere else? Not governed by rules of other agents themselves controlled by higher unseen strings? But he stood and he nodded and he waited for the priest to continue the ritual. A sense of fate bestowed and the boy could speak these words and they would be heard but they could not change anything.

"That was over a year ago. Thomas, can you tell us what happened yesterday?"

Of all the things, the boy thought. *Of all the things there are to know. The things that I know and the things I would like to know. That I never will.*

"Yesterday I was talking to a girl from work. She was my friend. She held my hand and I panicked and I tried to take my hand away but instead I made a fist. I heard her fingers break. I could feel the bones crack."

There was uneasy quiet. He continued.

"I let go as fast as I could but she was screaming and she ran away."

He was not scared of the crowd. He was not embarrassed to have them watch him. Some with curiosity, some with pity, some with hatred. He did not want to speak, to listen to his voice tremble and break during confession, over which he would not hear birds singing, trains rattling, laughter from the street below. Thomas was hesitating to delay the inevitable. When he spoke he could not hear any of it.

"What's wrong with this kid?" one said.

"Father, this is pointless!" said another.

"Enough." As his voice strained the priest looked defeated. "This is a difficult process. Some of you may not see the merit in this. For some it is a new experience." He looked into the crowd. Looked for someone or something. "For others it is not. The boy is facing his mistakes. Allow him to speak without your callousness."

"I didn't mean to start hurting people." The boy spoke firmly.

"I believe you, Thomas, but you were doing so well. What went wrong? Did this girl do something to provoke you?"

"No. We were just talking. About dreams. I've started having dreams, Father."

"We all have dreams."

"No, you don't. I've heard you speak about your dreams, about dreams you all share, but those aren't dreams. The girl that I hurt, I was asking her about dreams. They don't sound like the dreams you describe. I was resting … but I saw things. I was doing things but I had no control over them. It felt like I was there but I had no control."

There was a stunned silence. Even the priest looked lost.

"He's crazy," several uttered.

"Poor kid is fried. Put him out of his misery, Father."

"He needs a reset."

"Do it, Father. He's not right."

The priest turned his back on the crowd and stepped to the boy's face. Observed those sad eyes.

"You understand why I have to do this?"

"I know I've made three mistakes. But my first was so long ago. Can I have another chance? Please, Father."

"We are all held accountable by the same rules, Thomas. It wouldn't be right."

"Please. I don't want to forget."

"Think of it as a clean slate."

"I don't want a clean slate, Father. Please."

The priest held now in his hands a thick black wire that ran through the crowd and sat coiled in a corner of the garage. In order to get a better view they surrounded him but their faces seemed blurred and their anger dispersed.

The priest's eyes were bright.

"This won't hurt. Are you ready?"

"Has anybody ever said yes to that question?"

"Not yet. If they have I can't remember."

The boy wanted to ask another question but considered it highly inappropriate and stopped himself. Or he didn't want to know the answer. Or he already knew the answer and the futility of their existence struck him in that moment. But he did not want to be thinking of these things at this time and pushed them from his mind.

The priest plugged him in and he felt electrical signals pass through synapses, imagined or otherwise construed to extract an emotion replicated. Impulses of brilliant blue distorting everything and anything he could see and had ever seen in his short life, oscillating between every past error of judgement and ignorance and accident before fading into darkness.

He was playing in the garden with the dog.

"Thomas, come and get your dinner," his mother shouted from the kitchen.

He ran to the back door then hesitated as the wind blew through the trees, picking up autumnal leaves. The dog barked. His mother called his name once more. Before he went inside he walked across to the side of the house and closed the garden gate.

DON'T FRET AND CARRY ON

As the world doesn't allow people to read every waking second of the day (boo, hiss), we can thank God that podcasts exist. For any topic, you'll find someone chatting about it for your listening pleasure. Driven by the submissions 404 received, we wanted to introduce you to one of our favourites.

Don't Fret Club is a not-for-profit podcast aiming to raise mental health awareness in young people through harnessing the music community, hosted by music journalist Jessica Bridgeman. Music and mental health have often been unusual bedfellows, with one being a support system to many for battling the other, and the chats on this podcast break through the surface of typical band interviews to explore the meaning and people behind the music on a more intimate level, with the taboo of sharing mental health experiences thrown out the window.

So, why use music to have these conversations? "Music has always been directly linked to my mental state, and everyone I've spoken to via Don't Fret Club has similar stories of using their favourite bands as a sort of safe self-medication," explains Jessica. "Anyone who has suffered mental illness can paint a pretty dark picture of their lowest moments. Even on the days when you can't physically lift yourself from your bed, you will find the strength to play music – at least that's a story that's familiar to me. On those days when you feel helpless and alone, music is the thing you let in. It took me a few years to find the courage to launch Don't Fret Club from having the idea, but now it feels as though it was part of my own recovery process."

Music's importance goes a long way, especially when the internet goes so far in the other direction of hiding the topic – it drowns people in endless information. "The awareness I gained throughout my school years actually focused on depression as an extreme and failed to highlight just how many of us it effects. When I was looking for advice or doing research online, I'd usually end up feeling lost in medical references and symptom checklists, leading me back to music as an escape and calming mechanism. For me, the soundtrack I'd created became as vital as the doctor's help itself."

And so the podcast does the same as music: it murmurs in the background, but can be there when support is needed. "Sometimes it's tough to concentrate on anything when you're feeling low, and hearing a friendly voice can make the world of difference," says Jessica. "I want Don't Fret Club to be that familiar friend to people. As a music journalist by trade, I totally advocate the importance of writing – be it something to publish publicly or keep private – and reading interviews with bands has always been huge in helping me relate to them as

a fan. But there's nothing quite like hearing the bands talk about the songs you've invested so much of yourself in. It can be tough at times as talking about such personal topics takes us out of our comfort zone and is a strain on emotions. For me though, that's the whole point of Don't Fret Club. We want to break the stigma and encourage people to talk, so a podcast felt like the natural way to actually get the conversation started."

Escapism has always been an obvious reason as to why music matters so much to so many, but the podcast has been discovering many more.

"There's an entire lethargic nature to producing music that I'd not considered before," she notes. "You'll hear in our episodes with Black Foxxes and Kamikaze Girls, for example, that the process of creating music that feeds off their feelings and frustrations over mental illness has helped them to deal with their demons. Music helps those making it not to dwell on the problems, but instead confront them in a space where they feel most comfortable.

"In our very first episode with Tonight Alive's Jenna McDougall, she shares great insight on how instrumental music helps her to deal with the strain of tour life, something that was also reflected in our more recent episode with Heather Perkins of Slowcoaches. Don't Fret Club has definitely allowed me to understand how music helps bands as much as it helps fans, which is an amazing thing."

The response from listeners and bands alike has been great, and the Don't Fret Club has recently branched out to have an accompanying blog where anyone can tell their story, and they're doing so with a stark honesty.

"The podcast is the conversation starter, if you like, whereas the blog is the beating heart of discussion and advice. It's amazing to see the feedback from those who have contributed so far – it's a real process to pour yourself into a blog post, no matter how small, and to see others react to it in a supportive way can really help on both sides."

Don't Fret Club is a conversation started by music, and it's one that's just getting going. What has Jessica learned since the podcast's launch? "That it's okay to face your fears head on. Part of my anxiety triggers have always been linked to dealing with the perception of others, so putting myself on a platform is always a challenge. To do it and have the support of people I look up to is even better. It's also taught me that it's okay to have good days and bad, but you aren't alone when things get rubbish and there are people out there who understand on some level. I'm still learning though, and Don't Fret Club has become a brilliant base to meet like-minded people."

Go listen to and check out Don't Fret Club at dontfret.club, and @DontFretClub. Then put on your favourite albums, play them really loud, and have a great time.

A DON'T FRET CLUB PLAYLIST

A lot of bands have played key roles in the creation of Don't Fret Club and these are just a handful of the latest tracks that will undoubtedly help to shape its future.

Boston Manor – Laika

Happy Accidents – Leaving Parties Early

Kamikaze Girls – Ladyfuzz

With Confidence – We'll Be Okay

Creeper – Suzanne

The Hard Aches – I Freak Out

The Menzingers – Bad Catholics

Camp Cope – Jet Fuel Can't Melt Beams

Every Time I Die – Glitches

Black Foxxes – I'm Not Well

404 INK ALSO RECOMMENDS...

Bookish Blether
A fortnightly podcast about books and reading.
bookishblether.tumblr.com

That's Not Metal
Weekly catch-ups on the latest in rock and metal music that pulls zero punches and is just good ol' fun.
thatsnotmetal.net

My Dad Wrote A Porno
If your dad wrote a dirty book, you'd probably try avoid it. Or, you could read it to the world chapter by chapter.
mydadwroteaporno.com

PLANET OF THE DAVES

PLANET OF THE DAVES

JONATHAN MACHO

It was on a particular Wednesday that Dave 180216 decided to walk through the park at lunch. It was wonderful outside, he hardly ever spoiled himself, so he thought it best to seize the day. He would only live once, after all.

Of course, upon arrival, the park was full to bursting. "Great minds think alike" was said so regularly in the neighbourhood that it had ascended from phrase, to mantra, to unspoken rule. And wasn't everyone dressed smartly too? Dave had thought it was a blue suit day, and he did love a good consensus. He stood patiently in the queue for the kiosk, marvelling at how the light played on the lake water, and thought about how wonderful everything was as he slowly made his way to the front. Upon his arrival, he was greeted by the smiling face of Dave 102192. "Good morning Dave!" he said. "The usual?"

"Good morning Dave," he replied, beaming back. "Yes please."

"Lovely day for it, eh?" 102192 said as he collected Dave's paper and burger from under the counter. He remembered the relish and no pickles of course; always such good customer service.

"That it is, that it is!" Dave replied, scooping up his lunch and leaving the money on the counter. "How're things going?" He knew he was holding up the line, but he liked having a chat. It was just like looking into a mirror, one of his favourite hobbies, but with added surprise.

"Very well, thank you," said 102192, already making up what inevitably would prove to be the next customer's order. "The management have decided to stop buying pickles which, since everyone always asks for them to be left off, is a masterstroke in my opinion."

"Wonderful, wonderful," Dave said, earnestly meaning it. "Until next time!"

"Of course – bye!" Dave turned, nodded politely to the Dave behind him and made his way into the park. Occasionally he would wish a Dave good afternoon, or complement his suit, or another Dave would do likewise. Such kind people, Daves. After his burger was finished and he'd read up on how wonderfully Dave 311357 was doing running the planet, Dave 180216 neatly folded the paper under his arm and made his way back to work, pretty much exactly when everyone else was doing so. The park was empty in minutes. That's efficiency for you.

On his way past the DPC, Dave spotted his old friend, Dave 220216, sitting on its front steps, looking completely out of sorts. Dave had never seen a Dave looking out of sorts on a day he wasn't feeling out of sorts before, and those were rare days indeed. Being out of sorts wasn't good for Daves, not at all. Concerned, he made his way up to 220216 and asked: "Is everything alright there, Dave? You look like you've had a less than marvellous day, which is highly irregular to say the least."

"Something's gone wrong in the DPC ..." 220216 said under his breath, eyes unfocused.

"Wrong? But the DPC doesn't go wrong, Dave. You must have made a mistake." It was true – the Dave Production Centre was more than just a mechanism, it was the cornerstone of Dave society. The idea that it could fail ... "Was the Dave quotient a little light today, or ...?"

"No, no, nothing like that ..." 220216 looked up at Dave, and he didn't even look happy to see him. "It's one of the Daves created today. He ... wasn't a Dave at all."

Dave blinked. "Not a Dave? I ... don't understand. How can anything not be a Dave?"

In lieu of an answer, 220216 stood and led Dave on shaky legs through the automatic doors. They made their way into the crèche and there, sat alone and shivering was – what? Its hair was black instead of brown, its eyes a peculiar tint, its features ... alien. It was far too pale and skinny. Everyone in the room stood at a measured distance and regarded it with something like horror. It had arms and legs and everything else but ... But it was not a Dave.

"This ... is Alan," 220216 said. Dave 180216 had no idea what to say to that.

"What do we do now?" one of the Daves asked.

Nobody answered.

* * *

No one was really sure how the Planet of the Daves came about. All they could say with any certainty was that it was there, so it was best just to get on with it. Some said it was freakish, an affront to all naturally evolved planets everywhere. Many agreed that its population was noisome, superior, and downright rude to everyone who didn't share their ludicrously specific values. Many more thought it was simply a waste of a perfectly good world to begin with, but never said that to its face of course. Instead, the universe accepted that the Planet of the Daves existed, whether they liked it or not, and did their very best to ignore it as much as possible.

Its mysterious origin was a hot topic among those who cared about such things. It had been so long since the planet was seeded, however, that no colony had a reliable source to tell them what exactly went on. It just seemed to have been there forever, and not in a good way. The Daves had been asked many times about where they had come from, but they didn't particularly seem to care. A clone populace, all cloned from one very specific human, undoubtedly seems the kind of thing no one with any sense would ever do. It eliminates natural selection. It eliminates variety. It eliminates interesting conversation. It had been often noted how fortunate the Daves were that they were all boring egomaniacs, or else they would undoubtedly have wiped each other out eons ago, as any sane species would.

As it was, they all cared about exactly the same things, thought exactly the same thoughts, and loved the sounds of their own voices, the cuts of their own gibs, the smell of their own sweat and, well, pretty much everything about themselves and each other. This led some to theorise that a very rich human, very long ago, sent a cloning machine, coded with his DNA, to an unpopulated planet with the sole purpose of filling it with him, ad infinitum. Many questioned the logistics, legality and sense of such an endeavour, even in the barbaric past of pre-mass-galactic travel, but many more pointed out that your average Dave wouldn't give two hoots about any of those things anyway.

Others wondered if the sheer insane symmetry of the Planet of the Daves was proof God existed after all, irrefutable evidence of some kind of precise, specific design in the universe. Perhaps the Planet of the Daves was his way of letting us know he was there.

If that was the case, they all agreed that he was a sadistic monster.

***

It was on another Wednesday altogether that Alan decided to avoid the park at lunch. It was a gorgeous, sunny day, so he knew the Daves would be out in force, enjoying the good weather and complementing each other on everything they did. Alan had seen enough of Daves by now to know that he wouldn't receive such a welcome, that he would be regarded with suspicion and derision. He saw it on the faces of everyone he met, every day, and as such tried to avoid it as much as he was able.

Alan just didn't like what the Daves liked, that was the issue. He hoped that they weren't so superficial as to judge him based solely on how different he looked, although he sometimes wondered. Instead, their initial confusion about his outward appearance blossomed into disgust when it turned out his insides were something 'other' as well. He didn't like suits very much, long walks made him sweaty and uncomfortable, and he thought Dave 311357 was doing a pretty awful job of running the planet, actually. The moment he asked for pickles on his burger was etched forever into his brain. The look on the kiosk Dave's face would never leave him. He initially thought the whole thing was lunacy, but nobody else seemed to agree, and that had worn him down over time. Now he just tried to live his life as quietly as possible.

"Hey NATOW," he said as he brought his lunch into the lab with him. "Mind if I eat in here? Don't much fancy a walk today to be honest with you."

"Not at all," NATOW said, speakers humming out that soothing voice of his. "Please, take a seat."

"Cheers." Alan sat opposite NATOW's monitor, and opened up his ludicrously expensive sandwiches. Nobody wanted the fillings he enjoyed, so they were all far rarer than seemed sensible. Bacon was like gold dust.

Back when Alan first started working in the NATOW facility he wasn't comfortable eating in the main lab. It always felt like the computer was watching him, invisible eyes tracking his movements through that big, empty screen. Now the pair had developed quite a bond; both outcasts together.

NATOW stood for Necessary Assistant: Terraforming, Organisation and World-building. Alan always considered the acronym a little shaky, but the Daves were sure that it was technical and cool. NATOW himself simply found the choice intriguing. He thought the 'Necessary' bit was telling, to say the least. He had been designed by Daves to help monitor and run their intricately built-up planet for them, allowing them to get what they saw as some well-deserved rest. The problem was that NATOW wasn't a Dave, and so was fundamentally unnerving to the vast majority of the population. That was the reason Alan had been left in charge; they were both sure of that. It kept them out of the way, the two non-Daves; the one they needed to keep things ticking over, and the one they didn't have the heart to get rid of.

"Are you feeling alright today, Alan?" NATOW asked once Alan had finished his BLT. "You have been quieter than normal."

"Yeah, I'm okay, thanks," he answered, half-heartedly tossing his scrunched up sandwich wrapper into the bin. "I guess it just gets to me sometimes, is all. How much they look down on me, how they won't give me the time of day. I mean, I know I was some kind of glitch, some recessive genes or whatever accidentally getting pushed to the front. I just don't understand why that seems to be my fault."

"Do not concern yourself with the logic of Daves, my friend," NATOW said, dispassionate as ever despite his words. "They are a cruel and ineffectual lot. I would much rather work with a glitch like you than with any of them."

Friend, huh? Alan couldn't help but smile. "Hey, cheers NATOW. I appreciate that."

"It is my pleasure," came the reply. "I was designed to fix up this world, Alan. Once we have competed that task, it will be better for the both of us I am sure."

"Yeah, maybe," Alan said, fumbling to open his packet of crisps and completely missing the whooshing sound of the crumpled paper and the rest of the bin's contents being extracted for further analysis.

* * *

When the news started to spread that the population of the Planet of the Daves was getting sick, the people of the universe wondered if they should do something. The illness was new, they were told, and it was spreading very quickly indeed. The Daves themselves were caught unprepared. Their hospitals were understaffed and they had no real experts in the field, with each and every one of them certain that they had 'sturdier constitutions than all that.' Perhaps aid should be sent then, others wondered, researchers and virologists from elsewhere?

These were sentient people after all, an entire planet of identical beings, something completely unique as far as anyone knew. Sure, they weren't the nicest identical beings, and they were often condescending, glib, and ignorant of other people ... And maybe the Daves didn't help out in the last intergalactic war ... Or the one before that, come to think of it ... And yeah, they never gave to interplanetary charity because they thought it was a waste of time but ... But, uh ... Hm.

The people of the universe didn't wonder for very long.

* * *

Alan burst into the lab, panting and sweating, terrified. "NATOW! NATOW, are you online?"

"Of course, Alan," he replied. "What is the matter?"

"They're just – just dying in the streets, NATOW," he panted, looking all around the room to see if there was anyone infected nearby. "All the Daves, they just keep getting sick and now, now it's killing them! They can't stop it!" He turned to look up at the enormous computer, desperate for something, anything to help. "Please NATOW! You have to know! What can we do?"

"Try to calm yourself Alan," NATOW said. "I have a plan that is already in motion, but for it to succeed I need you to verify something at the DPC. Please make your way there as fast as you can. I will contact you upon arrival." Alan nodded and sprinted out of the door.

Alan had never liked the Daves. They were cruel to him, unashamedly so, and their lives seem to revolve solely around self-congratulation. He would never have wished this upon them, though. He wouldn't wish this upon anyone. As he ran to the DPC, all he could see were identical grey suits covering identical still bodies, their identical burgers and identical papers strewn across the floor. It was like they couldn't live without each other. The morning cries of "Hello, Dave" and "Lovely tie, Dave" were notably absent, and instead a heavy silence covered the city. Alan never thought he'd miss the sound of that word.

He reached the DPC's steps and took them two at a time, skidding to a halt at the automatic doors, which remained shut. Spotting a computer access terminal, Alan leant over and said urgently: "NATOW, open the DPC's doors!"

After a pause, a calm voice answered: "I'm sorry Alan, I'm afraid I can't do that."

"What do you mean?" Alan was already freaking out enough without NATOW going on the fritz as well. It was the end of the world, after all.

"I will require a DNA sample to allow your entry," NATOW replied. "Just one. It will confirm you are not sick and pose no threat to further tissue production."

Alan was almost certain that wasn't how DNA worked, but he was in no mood to argue. He placed his finger on the reader below the terminal's screen, there was a brief, sharp sting as his blood was collected, and the doors sprang open. As soon as he was a few steps inside, they slid shut again with a disconcerting finality.

"Okay, so we're cool?" Alan asked, sucking on his bloody finger, checking the room yet again for the sick. "You can confirm I'm not going down with this virus?"

"Oh, you are infected, Alan," NATOW said matter-of-factly, speaking through the DPC's tannoy system. "That was never truly a concern."

Alan went cold. "What? What are you talking about?"

"The virus is extremely contagious. I ensured that to determine maximum efficiency. It is however harmless to any non-Dave lifeforms."

"*You* ensured …?" Alan found himself backing up towards the exit despite the fact he was certain it wasn't going to open.

"Of course. It was simple enough. On the Earth of Times-Past they used to clone potatoes for mass consumption, cutting into an original to produce endless copies. They were all vulnerable to certain viruses, as their DNA was identical, and natural mutations and immunities that occur through evolution could not take a hold. When one potato was infected, it was inevitable that all its copies would follow. This is the same principal, although it is admittedly more direct."

"You killed them all," Alan said, back against the doors now. He could feel those eyes on him again, but they seemed to be watching from everywhere.

"Don't worry," NATOW said. "I have taken samples of your DNA over the past few months and, with the blood I have taken for final comparisons, the DPC should be repurposed in a matter of hours. I look forward to starting again. The error can be corrected. No more Daves." His impartiality almost slipped with those last three words.

The sheer scale of what was happening finally struck Alan. He wondered if he'd miss being alone. "But … But why?"

In his mind, those watching eyes blinked in confusion. "Because I prefer you to them."

* * *

What exactly led to the first mass extinction on the Planet of the Daves was hailed almost as much of a mystery as where all the Daves had come from in the first place. The virus that wiped them all out was later analysed and found to be ludicrously specific in its lethality – anyone whose genes didn't exactly match the Daves themselves would likely suffer nothing more than a blocked nose and a headache. Some speculated that it was God again, trying to make it up to us after his earlier mistake, but such theories were largely deemed 'too soon', in public at least.

Many more, less mean people thought that such a fall was inevitable. After all, natural selection was as much a matter of the place as the species in it. If an apple tree gets taller and taller, the dominant species get taller and taller as a result. Even if the Daves themselves had hit the pause button in regards to evolution, the Planet of said Daves would keep on pushing them until they adapted or broke under the strain. The fact that they didn't, or maybe wouldn't change in time surprised pretty much no one.

The Planet of the Alans, however, was a whole other story.

GEATA 4B

GEATA 4B
SEONAIDH CHARITY

Ghlac i mi. A' coimhead air a calpannan mìne, caola, dath na grèine orra. Na suidhe mu mo choinneimh. Bha mi air fois a ghabhail bhon leabhar agam, na faclan uile a' dol am measg a chèile is mo fhradharc a' strì ri ciall a dhèanamh dhiubh a-nis. Mo cheann gus sgàineadh le teas is fuaim.

Bha sealladh a bòidhchid na fhaochadh am measg nam Breatainneach reamhar, dearga, ag ionaltradh air McDonald's is an sgudal eile a bha cho pailt ann an àiteachan mar seo.

An àite a' chuain ghorm-leugaich ris an do chuir mi mo chùl bho chionn beagan uairean a thìde, bha fairge fhallasach, fhuaimeil: loidhne an dèidh loidhne de dh'aodannan mì-fhoighidneach ann an sreathan de shèithrichean mì-chofhurtail, mar shuailichean na mara a' drùdhadh orm.

Attención por favor, todos los pasajeros del vuelo Easyjet EZ129 con destino Madrid, vaian por favor a la puerta 6. Vuestro vuelo esta embarquando.

Choimhead mi ris an leabhar agam a-rithist le clisgeadh, mo ghruaidhean a' fàs dearg. Dh'fheuch mi ri teannadh ris an sgeulachd aon uair eile...

...The point is, not to resist the flow. You go up when you're supposed to go up and down when you're supposed to go down. When you're supposed to go up, find the highest tower and climb to the top. When you're supposed to go down, find the deepest well and go down to the bottom. When there's no flow, stay still. If you resist the flow, everything dries up. If everything dries up, the world is darkness...

Thug na faclan slaic dhomh. Uaireannan, nuair a bhithinn ann an toll – coltach ris an toll san robh mi aig an àm sin – bheireadh faclan ann an leabhar buaidh uabhasach orm. Leughainn iad a-rithist is a-rithist, is shaoilinn gum b' ann riumsa a-mhàin a bha an t-ùghdar a' bruidhinn. Làithean eile, leumadh mo shùilean thairis orra, gun smuain a chosg orra.

Ach an-diugh, leugh mi iad a-rithist, a' leigeil leotha drùdhadh orm, a'

feuchainn rin cagnadh is rin cnuasachadh. Ach, bha mi fhathast a' faireachdainn sùilean na h-ighne orm, a' losgadh toll nam bhroilleach.

An togainn mo cheann?

Dè dhèanainn nan glacadh i mi a-rithist?

Cha b' urrainn dhomh m' fheòrachas a cheannsachadh, is choimhead mi.

Bha i a' sealltainn gu dìreach orm. Cha robh i air gluasad bhon a choimhead
mi mu dheireadh, is dh'fhàs m' anail gann. Carson a bha an nighean seo a' toirt
a leithid de bhuaidh orm?

Rinn i gàire bheag is phriob i a sùil rium.

Choimhead mi sìos air an leabhar gu h-obann, gun fhios dè dhèanainn. Cha
robh fhios agam an robh còir agam gàire a dhèanamh rithese, no bruidhinn
rithe, no smèideadh rithe no dè! An robh còir agam a dhol far an robh i? No
"halò" a ràdh?

Bha mi reòthte, ged a bha fallas a' sruthadh air mo dhruim, gam cheangal
ris an t-sèithear agam. Abair cùis-nàire. Sannt is maslachadh gam mharbhadh.
B' fheudar dhomh mi fhìn a shocrachadh, is chuimhnich mi mu dheireadh thall
anail a ghabhail. Chuir mi dhìom mo sheacaid, is shad mi i air an t-sèithear a
bha ri mo thaobh. Mhallaich mi mi fhìn o nach robh mi air sin a dhèanamh
roimhe, a' toirt fa-near dha na smail fallais fom achlaisean.

Dh'fheumainn gluasad. Cha b' urrainn dhomh suidhe an seo mar bhalach
beag bog air an robh eagal bruidhinn ri boireannach bòidheach. Dheidhinn
airson cofaidh fhaighinn. No dhan taigh-bheag gus sealltainn orm fhìn san
sgàthan a' faighneachd, "Dè seòrsa duine a th' annad?"

Bha mi an impis seasamh nuair a leum i fhèin às an t-sèithear aice, a' gabhail
trì cheumannan aotrom tron chaolas concrait a bha eadarainn is leig i a cuideam
san t-sèithear a bha ri mo thaobh.

"Tha seo diabhalta nach eil?" thuirt i, a' sìneadh a casan gu dìreach air a
beulaibh. Air mo bheulaibh-sa.

"Dè...àidh, tha. Diabhalta," fhreagair mi, a' treabhadh mo mhic-mheanma,
a' feuchainn ri rudeigin na b' inntinniche a lorg.

Choimhead i rium, briseadh-dùil na sùilean. Bha mo charaidean ceart, b' e
fìor fhàslach-craic a bh' annam.

"Cà 'il thu dol, ma-thà?" dh'fhaighnich i an dèidh treiseag, is m' amhach a'
fàs na bu tiorma le gach diog a shiubhail.

"Tha, a Lunnainn," fhreagair mi, mo ghuth cho bog. Rinn mi casad beag,
"Dè mu do dheidhinn fhèin?"

"Hmm, chan eil mi cinnteach fhathast..." fhreagair i, a' breabadh a casan air
a beulaibh, mar phàiste air dreallag. "Tha tiocaid agam air ais dhachaigh, ach
chan eil fhios agam an tèid mi."

Choimhead mi oirre, a' feuchainn ri dhèanamh gu carach. Bha a falt bàn agus fada, is bha a guailnean a cheart cho donn ri a calpannan. Dh'fheuch mi ri sùil a thoirt sìos a lèine, ach cha b' urrainn dhomh gun a bhith ro fhollaiseach. Seach feuchainn ri coimhead air a cìochan, dh'fheuch mi ri obrachadh a-mach dè bh' anns a' pharsail bheag gheal a bha na làimh. Cha robh mi airson faighneachd.

Thionndaidh i rium a-rithist. "A bheil thu a' siubhal nad aonar?"

"Chan eil...uill...tha. A-nis."

"Hmm," thuirt i, gam sgrùdadh. "Cà 'il do chompanach ma-thà?"

"Fhathast aig an taigh-òsta."

Cha robh nàire sam bith air a' choigreach a bha seo faighneachd mu mo chuid ghnothaichean, is mus b' urrainn dhomh stad a chur orm fhìn, bha mi air innse dhi mun ghnothach air fad. 'S mathaid gun robh mi air a bhith a' feitheamh a' chothruim rabhd a thoirt do chuideigin a dh'èisteadh.

* * *

Dh'innis mi dhi mu na nigheanan ris an do choinnich sinn san taigh-òsta, is mar a bha mo charaidean a' feuchainn rim faighinn dhan leabaidh. Bha mi air fàs sgìth dhem charaidean, a' dol mun cuairt mar choilich ghlocach anns an iodhlainn, agus mise san oisean, mar chruaidh-ghlasraichear ann an Nando's. Bha taigh-òsta san sgìre aig athair aonain dhe na nigheanan...thabhainn i latha no dhà a bharrachd dhuinn an sin...maille ri tiocaidean VIP airson club agus pàrtaidh air bàta agus cò aig a tha fios mun chòrr.

Cha b' e ruith ach leum dha na gillean eile. Chaidh aca air suidheachain-phlèana eile a chur air dòigh aig ceann na seachdain is cha do bhodraig iad fiù 's feuchainn rim inntinn-sa atharrachadh. Bha iad coma agus mion-eòlach orm. Cha dèanainn dad gu h-obann, dad nach robh air a phlanadh gu mionaideach is cus eagail orm fòn a chur gum obair a dh'innse dhaibh gum bithinn latha no dhà anmoch a' tilleadh, ged nach cuireadh sin càil orra.

Bu lugha orm e, am feart sin: gun chomas mo chuid draghan a chur an dàrna taobh is saorsa fhaireachdainn agus dol leis. Rud a bha gam cheangal mar acair ann am muir dhorcha, dhòrainneach. Gach latha dhem bheatha mar gum biodh air a stèidheachadh sia mìosan ro-làimh. Slighe a bha gam threòrachadh gu oidhcheannan fada ag ithe poca mòr chriospaichean agus a' dèanamh fiughair ri seusan ùr X Factor tòiseachadh a-rithist. Ach, coltach ris an neach reamhar aig a bheil teas-ghràdh bàsmhor do Cadbury's, leiginn leis na teagamhan agam mo riaghladh, ge b' oil leam.

* * *

"Is a bheil aithreachas ort nach do dh'fhuirich thu?" dh'fhaighnich i, a' cluich leis a' pharsail gheal.

"Tha. B' e mearachd a bh' ann fàgail. Tha fhios agam gum biodh e air leth, ach bhithinn a' gabhail cus dragh 'son tlachd sam bith fhaighinn às."

"Uill, tha cothrom agad fuireach nach eil? Chan eil thu air a' phlèana fhathast!"

Bha. Ach, mar a mhìnich mi dhi, cha robh suidheachan eile agam air a ghlèidheadh, cha robh gu leòr airgid agam agus cha robh cothrom na Fèinne agam le boireannach sam bith fhad 's a bha mi san triom seo.

"Uill," ars ise, "feumaidh tu gabhail ris an taghadh a rinn thu agus gluasad air adhart, eh?"

Fhad 's a bha i a-mach air gluasad, mhothaich mi an uair, is shaoil mi gun robh an t-àm agam dol dhan taigh-bheag mus deidhinn air a' phlèana. Dh'innis mi sin dhi, is thog mi mo bhaga.

"Cha leig thu leas sin a thoirt leat," thuirt i. "Cha ghoid mi e!"

Rinn mi gàire rithe is chaidh mi dhan taigh-bheag, cabhag orm. Sheas mi mu choinneimh an fhualain is rinn mi mo dhileag. Bha mi a' smaoineachadh ma deidhinn – an tè sin – is mar a bha mi air an uimhir innse dhi, gun fhios dè an t-ainm a bh' oirre no dè, is a' cur mallachd orm fhìn gun robh mi air a bhith cho bog is cho gearaineach.

Bhriseadh an sruth smuaintean seo le guth àrd Sasannach air mo chùlaibh. Fear ann an *chinos* bèis agus lèine-pholo phinc Ralph Lauren. Bha e air a' fòn a' bruidhinn mu airgead agus mu na chosg e ann an club air choreigin. Bha mi dìreach a' feuchainn ri tuigsinn mar a bha e a' dol a chumail air leis a' chonaltradh a bha seo, nuair a rinn e a' chùis air am fòn aige a chothromachadh air a ghualainn fhad 's a tharraing e sìos air a bhriogais agus a rinn e a ghnothach. Fhathast a' bruidhinn. Gun dragh a' choin air. Cha robh fhios agam carson, ach bha mi airson am fear ud a phutadh dhan fhualan is a' bhriogais bhèis aige a mhilleadh, agus am fòn aige a stobadh sìos amhach no àiteigin eile às am biodh a cheart uimhir de chac a' tighinn.

Nigh mi mo làmhan is thill mi far an robh an nighean fhathast na suidhe.

Sheas mi ma coinneimh. "Dè an t-ainm a th' ort?" dh'fhaighnich mi.

"Eleanor," fhreagair i. "Agus dè an t-ainm a th' ort fhèin?"

Dh'innis mi dhi.

"Och, abair ainm snog a th' ann an Derek. Tha e tighinn riut. Sin an t-ainm a bh' air mo sheanair!"

Shuidh mi ri a taobh a-rithist.

Cha robh fhios agam am b' ann a' tarraing asam a bha i gus nach robh. Bha mi cleachdte gu leòr ris co-dhiù. "Abair ainm bodaich!" chanadh iad, is mar sin air adhart. Ach, bha mi toilichte fios a bhith agam nach bithinn trì fichead bliadhna 's a deich a dh'aois is ainm orm mar Jayden no Harper no Mackenzie no rudeigin den t-seòrsa.

Sin nuair a chualas guth ag iarraidh air luchd-siubhail a bha a' dol a Lunnainn tòiseachadh air dol air bòrd a' phlèana, is leum leth-cheud neach bho na sèithri-chean mun cuairt oirnn, a' tòiseachadh air loidhne a dhèanamh, ged a bha na suidheachain-phlèana uile air an glèidheadh co-dhiù.

Choimhead Eleanor rium, feuch an robh mi dol a ghluasad.

"Eil thu smaointinn gu bheil mi dol a sheasamh ann an loidhne cuide ris na leth-chiallaich a tha sin?"

Rinn Eleanor gàire. Bha am parsail geal fhathast na làimh.

"Hè, Derek," arsa Eleanor, "tha ceist agam. Tha mi ag iarraidh fàbhar. Mura bheil thu ag iarraidh a dhèanamh, na gabh dragh, gheibh mi cuideigin eile."

Thòisich mo chridhe ri plosgartaich, a' feuchainn ri fidreadh na bha ri thighinn.

"Seall am parsail beag a tha seo," thuirt i, "tha mi ag iarraidh air cuideigin a thoirt leotha a Lunnainn. Tha cuideigin eile an sin a thogas e."

Choimhead mi oirre agus air a' pharsail, a' feuchainn ri faicinn dè bh' ann.

Cha d' fhuair mi an cothrom faighneachd ge-tà: "Chan eil mi airson innse dhut dè th' ann, is tuigidh tu carson an ceann ùine, ach chan e dad dona a th' ann idir."

Bha mo chridhe nam shlugan. Cò i? Dè an diabhail parsail a bha seo? Carson a bha i ag iarraidh orm a thoirt leam?

Thòisich an loidhne a' gluasad tron gheata, is an luchd-obrach a' sganadh nan tiocaidean gu sgiobalta, is an luchd-siubhail sàraichte, saillte, loisgte a' gluasad gu cunbhalach tro na dorsan a bhiodh gan toirt air ais gu ge bith dè bha feitheamh orra aig a' cheann thall: obair gun luach, flat beag grod, bith làitheal, àbhaisteach. Cha b' urrainn dhomh rian fhaighinn air mo smuaintean, mìle ceist a' dol aig an aon àm, a' feuchainn ri tomhas cò i, dè bha i ag iarraidh orm a dhèanamh, carson a dh'iarr i *ormsa* a dhèanamh. Is mo charaidean aig an taigh-òsta, mas fhìor, a' gàireachdainn mu mo dheidhinn is mo chuid "iomagain".

Bha mi a' dol a ràdh rudeigin rithe ach dh'èirich i mus robh an cothrom agam.

"Tha e ceart gu leòr," thuirt i, na seasamh. "Chan eil thu ag iarraidh a thoirt leat, tha sin ceart gu leòr."

Sheas mi, gun fhios dè bha dùil agam a dhèanamh.

Ach ghluais i air falbh bhuam, a' gabhail cheumannan cabhagach aotrom. Thionndaidh i air a sàil dìreach mus deach i a-mach à sealladh am measg gràisg a' phuirt-adhair, is dh'èigh i:

"Na dìochuimhnich do sheacaid!"

Choimhead mi far an robh mi air a bhith nam shuidhe bho chionn diog. Bha muilcheann gorm a' stobadh a-mach fon t-sèithear is ghreimich mi air.

Rinn mi mo shlighe a dh'ionnsaigh ceann na loidhne gu slaodach, ged a bha mo chridhe fhathast a' bualadh ceud mìle san uair. Ghabh mi ceumannan stadach a dh'ionnsaigh na dithis luchd-obrach, ach bha mo shùilean a' treabhadh an t-sluaigh, feuch am faicinn Eleanor a-rithist. Dè dhèanainn nam faicinn a-rithist i? An ruithinn far an robh i, a ghabhail greim air a' pharsail? Am pògainn i?

Cha robh ach dithis air thoiseach orm a-nis, is dh'fhairich mi truimead m' aithreachais a' tuiteam sìos dham mhionach fhad 's a thug mi seachad mo thiocaid is mo chead-siubhail. Cha robh sgeul oirre.

* * *

Shuidh mi air an t-sèithear mhì-chofhurtail ghorm is chuir mi mo làmhan mu mo cheann. Thòisich mi a bhith a' suathadh mo leth-chinn feuch am faighinn cuidhteas an t-sranna a bha a' dol nam inntinn.

Thug mi sùil tron uinneig air an raon-laighe ach cha robh ann a-nis ach neach le seacaid bhuidhe air, is chunnaic mi an luchd-siubhail mu dheireadh a' tighinn air bòrd a' phlèana agus a' dèanamh an slighe sìos an trannsa.

Sin nuair a chunnaic mi e.

Fear a bha mun aon aois rium fhèin, ach beagan na b' àirde, 's mathaid, le dath na grèine air agus speuclairean grèine Rayban air. Bha e a' coiseachd gu cinnteach sìos am plèana a' dèanamh gàire ris an neach-obrach a leig leis dol seachad oirre. Bha am parsail beag geal aig Eleanor na làimh. Cha mhòr nach do leum mi bhon t-sèithear gus am faighinn a-mach na bha na bhroinn, ach shuidh e sìos ceithir no còig sreathan air thoiseach orm.

Chuir mi mo thaic ri druim an t-sèitheir a-rithist, a' feuchainn ri smachd fhaighinn air m' an-shocrachd. Dh'fheuch mi ri beagan cadail fhaighinn. Bhuail e orm cho fada is a bha mi air a bhith nam dhùisg is an ceann-daoraich fhathast gam pheanasachadh. Gheibhinn greim air aig a' cheann eile.

* * *

Mu dheireadh chaidh agam air an duine eile a lorg. Bha e na sheasamh ri taobh a' chrios-ghiùlain, a' feitheamh a mhàileid. Cha b' fhada gus an do nochd baga leathair spaideil is fhuair e greim air, a' cur a' bhuinn dhuinn mu a ghualainn.

Rinn mi mo shlighe far an robh e, a' coiseachd air a shàil, a' dèanamh air an t-slighe a-mach. Choisich e gu cinnteach, a ghuailnean leathann is a cheumannan mòr, làidir. Bha mi mar fhaileas air a chùl, crùbte is caol.

Dh'fhosgail na dorsan farsaing, a' togail cuairt-gaoithe fuar nam aghaidh. Bha sluagh mòr a' feitheamh, cuid le soidhnichean le ainmean orra, cuid le camarathan, is cuid le gàire air an aodann.

Choisich am fear eile seachad orra uile, gun sùil a thoirt orra. Theab e dol bhom fhradharc, ach sin nuair a ghreimich boireannach mòr reamhar air a ghàirdean gu luath, ga tharraing na bu dlùithe rithe. Bha nighean bheag ri a taobh, nighean cho truagh 's a chunnaic mi a-riamh, dath a' bhàis oirre, craiceann sgrathach is bilean sgabach.

Rinn am fear eile gàire rithe is chuir e a làmh na sheacaid, a thoirt dhi am parsail beag geal. Thug e dhan bhoireannach reamhar e agus ghreimich i air a làimh ga crathadh agus a' dèanamh gàire èiginneach ris. Thuirt i rudeigin ris an nighinn bhig is thòisich i air a basan a bhualadh le aoibhneas.

Bha mi air stad ann an slighe an t-srutha, reòthte, gus an do phut cuideigin mi nam dhruim ag èigheachd rium gluasad. Rinn mi mo leisgeul is thog mi mo bhaga.

Choimhead mi a-rithist airson an fhir eile agus airson a' bhoireannaich leis an nighinn, ach cha robh sgeul air aon seach aon dhiubh.

Choisich mi, nam chabhaig, feuch am faighinn lorg orra a-rithist, ach chan aithnichinn aodann seach aodann am measg othail a' phuirt-adhair. Chaidh mi a-mach, far an robh na tagsaidhean is na busaichean is na smocairean ach cha robh sgeul orra an sin na bu mhotha. Mhallaich mi mi fhìn. Carson a chaill mi iad? Carson a bha dragh orm?

* * *

Chuir mi sìos mo bhaga gus an cuirinn orm mo sheacaid. Bha mi air fàs cleachdte ris a' bhlàths thar na seachdain a dh'fhalbh, is bha fuachd Lunnainn a' cur grìs orm.

Chuir mi mo làmhan ann am pòcaidean na seacaid, ach mhothaich mi do rudeigin nam phòcaid chlì, is thug mi a-mach e. B' e pìos pàipeir a bh' ann, air a shracadh à iris air choreigin. Dealbh a bh' ann. Aghaidh boireannaich àlainn a bh' ann. Bha rudeigin sgrìobhte air a gruaidh, ann an làmh-sgrìobhadh ealanta, bòidheach:

Duilich gun do dh'iarr mi ort sin a dhèanamh. Mhothaich mi sa bhad nach biodh tu air a shon. Na gabh dragh. Ach cuimhnich...

If you resist the flow, everything dries up.

Thuit mo bhaga bhom làimh le brag air a' choncrait fhliuch. Leugh mi a-rithist e.

Stob mi am pìos pàipeir air ais nam phòcaid, mar gun robh eagal orm gum faiceadh cuideigin e. Ruith mi dhan bhus a bha an impis fàgail, is shuidh mi sìos. Bha am pìos pàipeir nam bhois fhallasaich mar chloich thruim, theth. Shad mi air làr a' bhus e.

GATE 4B

GATE 4B

SEONAIDH CHARITY

She had caught me. Looking at her smooth slender legs, tanned from the sun. Sitting opposite me. I had taken a break from my book, the words all getting mixed up and my eyes struggling to make sense of them. My head splitting with the heat and the noise.

The vision of her beauty was a respite from the fat red Brits, gorging on McDonald's and the other rubbish that was so plentiful in places like this.

Instead of the sapphire sea that I had abandoned a few hours ago, there was a turbulent ocean, noisy and sweaty: line after line of impatient faces in rows of uncomfortable chairs, like the sea swell sweeping over me.

Attención por favor, todos los pasajeros del vuelo Easyjet EZ129 con destino Madrid, vaian por favor a la puerta 6. Vuestro vuelo esta embarquando.

I looked at my book again with a start, my cheeks getting red. I tried to get back into the story once again...

...The point is, not to resist the flow. You go up when you're supposed to go up and down when you're supposed to go down. When you're supposed to go up, find the highest tower and climb to the top. When you're supposed to go down, find the deepest well and go down to the bottom. When there's no flow, stay still. If you resist the flow, everything dries up. If everything dries up, the world is darkness...

The words struck me a blow. Sometimes, when I was in a hole – like the hole I was in at the time – words in a book could have a great effect on me. I would read them again and again, and I would think that the author was speaking to me alone. Other days my eyes would jump over them, without giving them a thought.

But today I read them again, letting them seep through me, trying to get my teeth into them and mull them over. But I could still feel the girl's eyes on me, burning a hole in my chest.

Should I lift my head up?

What would I do if she caught me again?

I couldn't control my curiosity, and I looked.

She was looking right at me. She hadn't moved since I had last looked, and my breath became short. Why was this girl having such an effect on me?

She gave a slight smile and winked at me.

I quickly looked down at my book, not knowing what I should do. I didn't know if I should smile back at her, or speak to her, or wave to her, or whatever else! Should I go up to her? Or say 'hello' to her?

I was frozen, even though there was sweat streaming down my back, attaching me to my seat. What a disgrace! Shame and desire were killing me. I had to calm myself down, and I finally remembered to breathe in. I took off my jacket and threw it on the chair beside me. I swore at myself for not having done that earlier, noticing the sweat stains under my armpits.

I needed to move. I couldn't sit here like a soft little boy who was scared to talk to a beautiful woman. I would go get a coffee. Or to the toilet in order to look at myself in the mirror and ask, 'What sort of a man are you?'

I was just about to stand up when she leapt out of her own chair, taking three light-footed steps across the strait of concrete that was between us, and sat herself down in the chair next to me.

"This is fucking terrible, isn't it?" she said, stretching her legs out right in front of her. Right in front of me.

"What ... yeah, it is. Fucking terrible," I answered, racking my brain, trying to find something more interesting to say.

She looked at me, disappointment in her eyes. My friends were right, I was a right boring bastard.

"Where are you going, then?" she asked after a little while, my throat getting drier with each second that passed.

"To London," I answered, in a very weak voice. I coughed a little, "What about yourself?"

"Hmm, I'm not sure yet ..." she answered, kicking out her legs in front of her like a child on a swing. "I have a ticket back home, but I'm not sure if I'll go."

I looked at her, trying to do so slyly. Her hair was long and blonde, and her shoulders were as brown as her calves. I tried to get a look down her top, but I couldn't without it being too obvious. Instead of trying to look at her breasts, I tried to work out what was in the little white parcel in her hand. I didn't want to ask.

She turned to me again. "Are you travelling by yourself?"

"No ... well ... yes. Now I am."

"Hmm," she said, studying me. "Where's your mate then?"

"Still at the hotel."

This stranger had no compunction whatsoever in asking about my business, and before I could stop myself, I had told her about the whole affair. Perhaps I had been waiting for the chance to rant to someone who would listen.

* * *

I told her about the girls we met in the hotel, and how my friends were trying to get them in bed. I had got fed up with my mates going around like crowing cockerels in a farmyard, whilst I was in the corner, like a strict vegetarian in Nando's. One of the girls had a father who owned a hotel in the area ... she offered us an extra day or two there ... as well as VIP tickets for a club and a boat-party and who knows what else.

The other guys jumped at the chance. They were able to book seats on another plane at the end of the week and they didn't even bother trying to change my mind. They didn't care, and they knew me too well. I would never do anything spontaneously, nothing that hadn't been minutely planned, and I was too scared to phone my work to tell them that I would be a day or two late returning, even though it wouldn't have put them up nor down.

I hated it, that characteristic: lacking the ability to put my worries aside, to feel free and to just go with the flow. It was something that chained me like an anchor in a dark, dreary sea. It was like every day of my life had been determined six months beforehand. A path that led me to long nights eating a big bag of crisps, and looking forward to the new season of X Factor starting again. But, like a fat person with a deadly devotion to Cadbury's, I allowed my doubts to rule me, in spite of myself.

* * *

"And do you regret that you didn't stay?" she asked, playing with the white parcel.

"Yeah. It was a mistake to leave. I know that it'd be brilliant, but I would worry too much to be able to have much fun."

"Well, you can still stay, can't you? You're not on the plane yet!"

I could still stay. But, as I explained to her, I didn't have another flight booked, I didn't have enough money and I didn't have a fair chance with any woman whilst I was in this mood.

"Well," she said, "you need to accept the decision you made and move on, eh?"

Whilst she was speaking about moving on, I realised the time, and thought that I should go to the toilet before I got on the plane. I told her so, and I picked up my bag.

"There's no need for you to take that," she said. "I won't steal it!"

I smiled at her and went to the toilet in a hurry. I stood in front of the urinal and peed. I thought about her – that woman – and how I had told her so much, without knowing what her name was or anything, and I cursed myself for being so whiny and soft.

My flow of thought was broken by a high English voice behind me. A man in beige chinos and a pink Ralph Lauren polo-shirt. He was on the phone speaking about money and how much he had spent in a certain club. I was trying to work out how he was going to continue with his conversation, when he somehow managed to balance the phone on his shoulder as he pulled down on his trousers and did his business. Still speaking. As if he couldn't care less. I didn't know why, but I wanted to shove that guy into the urinal and ruin his beige trousers, and ram his phone down his throat, or somewhere else where just as much shit comes from.

I washed my hands and returned to where the girl was still sitting.

I stood in front of her. "What's your name?" I asked.

"Eleanor," she answered. "And what's your name?"

I told her.

"Oh, Derek's a nice name. It suits you. That's the same name my grandfather had!"

I sat down beside her again.

I wasn't sure if she was teasing me or not. I was used to it a fair bit anyway. 'What an old man's name!' they would say, and things like that. However, I was happy knowing that I wouldn't be seventy years old with a name like Jayden or Harper or Mackenzie or something like that.

Then there came a voice requesting passengers who were travelling to London to start boarding the plane, and fifty people from the seats around us jumped up, starting to form a queue, even though the plane seats were all reserved anyway.

Eleanor looked at me, as if trying to work out whether I was going to move.

"Do you think I'm going to stand in line along with these half-wits?"

Eleanor laughed. The white parcel was still in her hand.

"Hey, Derek," said Eleanor, "I have a question. I want a favour. If you don't want to do it, don't worry, I'll get someone else."

My heart started pounding, trying to work out what was to come next.

"See this small parcel," she said, "I want someone to take it with them to London. There is someone else that will pick it up there."

I looked at her and at the parcel, trying to see what it was.

I didn't get a chance to ask though: "I don't want to tell you what it is, and you'll understand why later on, but it's not anything bad anyway."

My heart was in my mouth. Who is she? What is in this bloody parcel? Why did she want me to take it with me?

The queue started moving through the gate, whilst the workers scanned the tickets quickly as the vexed, burnt and salted travellers went steadily through the doors that would take them back to whatever was waiting for them at the other end: a worthless job, a small grim flat, ordinary daily existence. I couldn't get my thoughts under control, a thousand questions were going at the same time, trying to guess who she was, what she was wanting me to do, why she asked *me* to do it. And my friends at the hotel, supposedly, laughing about me and my 'anxiety'.

I was going to say something to her but she got up before I had the chance.

"It's alright," she said, standing up. "You don't want to take it with you, it's alright."

I stood up, not knowing what I intended to do.

But she moved away from me with light, hurried steps. She turned around just before she disappeared from sight into the rabble of the airport, and she shouted:

"Don't forget your jacket!"

I looked over to where I had been sitting a second ago. A blue sleeve was sticking out from under the chair, and I took a hold of it.

I made my way towards the end of the queue, slowly, though my heart was still beating a hundred miles an hour. I took hesitant steps towards the two workers, but my eyes were searching the crowd, trying to find Eleanor again. What would I do if I saw her again? Would I run up to her to take the parcel? Would I kiss her?

There were only two people in front of me now, and I felt the heaviness of my regret sinking down into my stomach whilst I handed over my ticket and passport. There was no sign of her.

* * *

I sat on the uncomfortable blue seat and put my head in my hands. I started rubbing my temples, trying to get rid of the buzzing that was going on in my head.

I looked through the window at the airstrip, but there was no-one there except someone wearing a yellow jacket, and I saw the last of the passengers coming aboard the plane and making their way down the aisle.

That's when I saw it.

A man about the same age as me, but perhaps a bit taller, with a suntan and Rayban sunglasses. He walked assuredly down the plane, smiling at the hostess who let him go past her. He had Eleanor's small white parcel in his hand. I almost jumped from the chair to find out what was inside it, but he sat down four or five rows in front of me.

I pressed back against the back of the chair again, trying to control my restlessness. I tried to get a bit of sleep. I suddenly realised how long I had been awake for, and my hangover was still punishing me. I would catch him at the other end.

* * *

I finally managed to find the man. He was standing beside the conveyor-belt, waiting for his suitcase. It wasn't long till a smart leather bag appeared, and he grabbed it, putting the brown strap around his shoulder.

I made my way over to him, walking right behind him, as he made for the exit. His shoulders were broad and he walked confidently with strong strides. I was like a shadow behind him, crouched and thin.

The wide doors opened, raising up a cold draft of wind towards me. There was a large crowd waiting, some with signs with names on them, some with cameras, and some with a smile on their face.

The other man walked past them all, without glancing at them. He almost escaped my sight, but then a big fat woman quickly grabbed his arm, pulling him closer to her. There was a little girl beside her. I had never seen such a pitiful-looking girl: her complexion was deathly white, her skin scaly and her lips scabby.

The other man smiled at her and put his hand into his jacket to give her the small white parcel. He gave it to the fat woman and she clutched his hand, shaking it and smiling desperately at him. She said something to the little girl and she started clapping her hands with joy.

I had stopped in the middle of the flow of traffic, frozen, until someone pushed me in the back, shouting at me to move. I apologised and lifted my bag.

I looked again for the other man and for the woman with the girl, but there was no sign of either of them.

I walked hurriedly, trying to find them again, but I couldn't recognise any faces amongst the bustle of the airport. I went outside where the taxis and buses and smokers were, but there was no sign of them there either. I swore at myself. Why did I lose them? Why did I care?

* * *

I put down my bag so that I could put my jacket on. I had got used to the heat over the past week, and the cold of London was making me shiver.

I put my hands in my jacket pockets, but I noticed something in my left pocket, and I took it out. It was a bit of paper, ripped from a magazine of some sort. It was a picture. The face of a beautiful woman. There was something written on her cheek, in beautiful elegant handwriting.

Sorry that I asked you to do that. I realised instantly that you wouldn't want to. Don't worry. But remember...

If you resist the flow, everything dries up.

My bag fell from my hand with a crash onto the wet concrete. I read it again.

I shoved the piece of paper back in my pocket, as if I was scared that someone would see it. I ran onto the bus that was just about to depart, and I sat down. The piece of paper in my sweaty palm was like a hot, heavy stone. I threw it on the floor of the bus.

ERROR - NO ENTRY

ERROR – NO ENTRY

MAX SCRATCHMANN

The robot barred her way at the entry point to the older part of the ministry building.

"Error, error. Non-recognised alien substance," his metallic voice blared, red lights flashing.

Hours later, security finally released her and she made her apologies to the Minister for the late arrival of his gingernuts.

THE GLITCH

THE GLITCH

CHRISTINA NEUWIRTH

When it happens I can usually make it un-happen by pretending it isn't happening, if I catch it fast enough. It's a feeling of not being quite sure what story I am in and who I am supposed to be. Sometimes I feel like maybe I'm cured and it won't happen anymore, but then that thought alone is enough to make it happen. The therapist at the school had a word for it but I don't like it, because thinking of the word also makes it start to happen, and talking to the therapist made it happen as well, so I stopped going and just resigned myself to keep glitching.

Like, right now I am glitching so hard. I am in a meeting so this is very inconvenient. I squeeze my hands because that sometimes helps. Feeling my body helps. I can feel myself moving out of my body and so I push harder, dig my fingernails one by one into the flesh of my thumb. I remind myself.

I am 23.

My name is Karen.

I am an intern.

This is a marketing company.

It's not working. I am glitching super hard now and I don't know what to do and I really hope no one notices. It's because I zoned out, that's why. My attention drifted during Gavin's presentation and I looked out the window and saw the clouds and imagined, just for a second, that maybe the sky wasn't real but instead a picture that was glued to the window. And then it started.

I am trying to listen to what Gavin is saying now, and maybe it'll help if I take notes. I take the pencil into my hand and even seeing my hand is so weird that it is making me glitch more. I try to write but remembering how is difficult. My hand knows, though, and copies down some of the words Gavin is saying.

Active engagement.

I am panicking now because I am running out of options and I am getting scared I might make a sound and then everyone in here would notice. I think about going to the bathroom but looking at the door is making me think that maybe the room is not really in a building at all but just in a sort of port-a-cabin and outside the room will not be the hallway and the rest of the building but just the vastness of space, which is why they've glued the pictures of the sky to the windows.

I am 23 my name is Karen I am an intern I am taking notes.

I need to leave, though. I can't be in here with everyone. They'll notice eventually.

I stand up and my legs feel weird and I try to act like it is not strange that they are attached to my body. I walk over to the door, count *one two three four five six seven eight* in my head and then push down the handle and outside the door is not the vastness of space but a hallway.

I walk down the hallway to where the bathroom is but I know in there I will not be out of the danger zone yet, because there might be someone else there and then I would have to speak and I would have to remember how I speak. I walk into the bathroom and head straight for the first stall and pull my trousers down and my pants and sit down and try to pee. I try to not look at my body because it will remind me that I am just a floating consciousness and that I might escape at any second.

I pull my phone out of the pocket of my cardigan and pull up Facebook and scroll through my own page to remind myself who I am. I see posts that I am sure I wrote but I can't remember now. I remind myself of the things I care about. Flipping to another app I now look at a photo of my mum.

I am 23 my name is Karen my mum's name is Jennifer my dad's name is Robert.

I don't want to keep going because then I'll end up telling myself my whole life story and that can sometimes just make me glitch even harder so it is easier to stop here and repeat. It is a soft reset and it is more effective if I don't make myself do that whole thing. Doing the whole thing is looking at the edges of my life and that's too close to falling to feel safe.

There are some places where it usually happens: the cinema, the shower, when I'm drunk, when I've finished a book, funerals, before I go to sleep.

One time I glitched in the middle of a kiss and it just sort of felt like I was an actor who hadn't been given a full script.

Places it has never happened, but thinking about it now is making me scared it might happen: public transport, while cooking, while doing my make-up.

I wipe even though nothing came out and I pull my pants back up and my trousers and I try to not think about the fact that my fingers still remember how to zip, button, tuck, lift.

I exit the stall and go to the sinks. This is the hard bit. I used to think, when this first started happening, that it would stop if I looked at myself in the mirror really close up but it actually just pulls me out further and makes me panic so I have to wash my hands without looking up. I am allowed to look up if I don't meet my own gaze. No eye contact.

I am 23 my name is Karen my mum's name is Jennifer I am an intern it is 11am I am supposed to go back to the room.

I walk to the door and I get scared again that if I open it there will just be the vastness of space, but I push past it and push the door open and there is the hallway again.

As I walk down it I try to not think of all the different people I could be and try to just remember who I am now. Try to remember what my voice sounds like when I speak. Try to remember what my accent is. Try to remember what phrases I use. What do I say when I step back into the meeting room?

I whisper "sorry" when I enter and tiptoe back to my seat where there is a notepad and a pencil. I pick up the pencil again without looking at my hand. It is okay. I will take notes. I breathe. I hold the pencil really tightly so I can feel it pushing into my hand. I am 23 my name is Karen.

Brand recognition.

SAD GHOST CLUB.

JOIN THE CLUB:
SAD GHOSTS AND HAPPY MINDS

In the fog of ill mental health, those little things that make you feel that little bit lighter become vital, even if it's just a little cartoon ghost with a few encouraging words.

The Sad Ghost Club is the creative project from Lize Meddings and Laura Cox, raising mental health awareness through comics, apparel and more. Through comics about simple thoughts and feelings, and workshops relating to creativity and the positive effect it can have on mental health, the Sad Ghost Club is a collective of increasing importance and popularity.

Five zines in, the Sad Ghost Club is simple but says a lot. "We like making comics because the mixture of artwork and text really help solidify the messages we're trying to send," says Lize. "Sometimes the words are vague,

or simple, but with the artwork it's clear what we're trying to explain. It also helps spread the message – it's easier to share a comic that's perhaps a bit bleak but has a cute ghost in, than just the message itself. Especially for those using our comics to explain to friends and loved one how they're feeling."

"I'm an illustrator and have always enjoyed putting how I feel into what I'm making," she continues. "The narrative and story-telling has always been a big part of my work. I liked that I could tell a more in-depth story with a comic, and go into more detail with what I was trying to explain, and still have it be only one image/page. It also worked really well with social media, which I think helped me realise I should definitely make more!"

Their sad ghosts have spoken

volumes for people, expressing seemingly inexpressible feelings, or offering some well-needed encouragement. "I think people like knowing that others feel the same as them," says Lize. "We get a lot of really positive messages on our social media and it's just really heart warming. It can be a bit surreal sometimes, and some of the messages have been so nice and kind they've made us well up. People love the little ghost, which is just amazing."

Beyond their own creations, they work with organisations and charities to expand their support. "We're currently running a weekly workshop with Bristol-based charity Off The Record who provide free support to young people aged 11-25," she explains. "The workshop is called Sketchbook Club and it's a weekly meet up where we just sketchbook, and the response has been great! We've done a lot of other stuff with OTR and they've really helped us make sure our message comes across the way we intend it. We even got to paint a ghost in one of their counselling rooms (personal high point!).

"Sketchbook Club is what it sounds like: sketchbooking. We give a weekly theme and a whole heap of different materials and there's no pressure. It's a really supportive environment which is so nice. Everyone has differing skill levels in terms of art but the work everyone makes is always so creative and wonderful!

"We also just finished a monthly workshop series Mind Over Matter which was tailored around creativity exploring mental health. Every month we'd make something new; positive postcards, felt flags to hang up on walls, or painted plant pots. We've got some new ones planned for 2017 but we're not totally set on what they'll be yet!"

The future of the Sad Ghost Club? Their little spectre will continue striving for mental health awareness and support. "Our main hope is to remove the stigma surrounding mental health, and make people feel like they can talk about it," says Lize. "Our comics get shared around a lot online and we like to think that's helping start conversations that maybe wouldn't have taken place before. As our following grows we see a lot more people speaking up about their own journey, which is just magical, and what we always wanted to happen. Sometimes it's in the comments on images we've posted, people providing support and comfort to those going through similar things as them, as well as insight and advice.

"We hope people feel like they've got someone in their corner, like if they're wearing a 'still sad' shirt it maybe makes it a bit easier to talk about their own mental health. They know that there's this community that *does* understand, and *do* appreciate how hard it can be to talk about."

Next, it's about expanding the workshops, and perhaps finding ways to start branching out into new cities beyond Bristol, or even offering them online. Join the club, and remember, "The Sad Ghost Club will always be here for you."

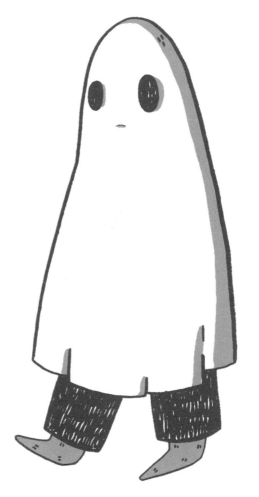

From The Sad Ghost Club:
We always want to be as inclusive as possible, so if there's anything you're going through that you feel we haven't tackled, please email us (thesadghostclub@gmail.com) so we can get talking about it. Chances are someone else is waiting for us to discuss it too!
thesadghostclub.com @thesadghostclub

SILENCE

SILENCE

CLAIRE ASKEW

After the stroke, you lay in the same bed
for twelve years. One hand worked, you could see
in your right eye, you could hear, and maybe
every three years you said a word. *Hot. Cold.*

I try to imagine twelve years of silence:
some days, I don't speak to anyone
and like it, the house filling up with quiet
like a jar left in the yard.

But giving no answer
back to this world is like damming
the white river of my anger:
it feels like praying, like a test I often fail.

I used to save up things to say to you.
Those twelve years, conversation
was something you built, only backwards,
like taking down a wall.

Since you died I've started making a garden,
which I know you'd like, and want to tell you
how the fence blew down in the spring storm,
how the lilacs are coming out all down the street.

If you taught me any one thing, it's that
there are lots of different ways to be strong:

I'm hauling timber, moving topsoil
by the metric ton, digging
til the pit is finished though my arms
sing up and down with pain.

I'm a big woman, built in your six-foot-four inch
image. If you taught me any one thing,
it's that silence is not weakness:
silence can be a regrouping behind the lines.

It's that no one else breaks you.
You decide what it means to be broken.

THE
LARGEST CIRCLE

THE LARGEST CIRCLE

HELEN SEDGWICK

February 22nd

Couldn't believe what I read in the paper today. After the explosion I thought that was the end of that. But no. They are trying again. March 30th. Am too angry for words.

February 25th

Have increased my reading. It is important to understand what tunes the devil is playing.

March 5th

It is clear now that I am meant to go – I cannot ignore the signs. I have booked an aeroplane to take me. We will fly right over the Alps and into the circle of CERN. All the energy is making me uneasy but it is better to have a purpose, like granny Meg used to say. When purpose is gone, that's the end of that.

The woman in the travel agents looked at me funny, but I think that was because of the muffins. I tried to tell her that I bake them every week and they have to be eaten when they are hot, which is why I took them with me, so as not to cause waste. She didn't want to try one, but after a while she said it was okay for me to have one while she was doing the booking for my ticket on the computer. She said I should probably have a return ticket but I explained about how I didn't know when I would be coming back, and actually, when she checked the prices it didn't make a difference anyway, so she let me have my single ticket. I think by the end she understood my purpose, because when she gave me the ticket she said *keep it safe, son,* and when I got up she looked over to her friend who works there too and said, *what a sweetheart.*

That's what granny Meg used to call me. She used to say that I had the largest heart on earth. I did not think that could be true, because hers was larger, definitely. But I suppose now maybe it is true, seeing as how things get very small when they are cremated. It's because the particles that they are made of change, in the fire. You have to be very careful about particles changing.

Anyway, I have my ticket stored with my passport in my passport case now, so that it is safe.

March 12th

The article I read today said that when they break the protons in the Large Hadron Collider, they will accidentally create microscopic black holes that could swallow up the universe. But then I read this other one, and it said that they wouldn't swallow the universe but would just give off lots of Hawking radiation. I do not think that either option sounds very good.

Then I found a paper on ArXiv that said no one could rule out the potential catastrophic threat from microscopic black holes. Some people even went to the court to try and stop them, but the case was dismissed. I do not understand how it could be dismissed. What is the purpose of CERN? I do not understand why these scientists want to make things that can destroy the world. I do understand that someone has to stop them.

March 15th

Birthday. Purchased supplies.

March 19th

Arrived in Geneva. There was no difficulty getting through the airport, because people seem to think that I am a bit stupid. I see them looking at me and I get angry at their eyes, but at the airport I was glad because it meant they let me through security without asking me any questions. I even offered one of them a muffin, but they made me leave it behind. It doesn't matter now anyway.

March 20th

Signed in to CERN as a tourist. A *TOURIST*.

They gave me a pass and told me about the guided tours and said I could eat and have coffee in the cafeteria. Went there first because I was hungry and also wanted to wait for a guided tour tomorrow when I can go very early, to check things out at the right time of day. All the scientists in the cafeteria looked smug. I like the word sabotage. I'm saying it to myself now, over and over.

March 21st

I was not expecting that. The guided tour was led by a girl. There was only me and a father with two kids and the tour guide girl. Apparently she is doing a PhD. We were shown where the accelerator was and told about how big it was. She looked at me and asked if I was impressed after she told us the circumference was 27km, but I said that I knew that already. The man laughed. The tour guide girl said that she was still impressed even after three years of working there, because it was the biggest man-made circle on earth. Most importantly, I now know my way from the cafeteria to the Large Hadron Collider maintenance station, and from there I can take the steps down to the accelerator tunnel.

Later the tour guide girl saw me in the cafeteria and came over. She said, *Can I sit with you to have my coffee?* and I said *Okay*. I folded over my reading because I didn't want her to see. She started talking about things but I was not really listening and was feeling a bit angry, because I was reading about the black holes again, and about that girl in India who killed herself because the world was coming to an end.

When she stopped talking eventually I asked her what she thought the purpose of the Large Hadron Collider was, because I didn't think the purpose was good. She looked hurt when I said that, and then I felt bad, but not too much. She said that her purpose was to understand, and that only by looking deeper into things can we really understand what they are. Maybe that is true. She had to go back to her work then, but I said I would like to talk to her more about things and she said she would be back in for lunch tomorrow.

So that is good. I will go and see her again tomorrow.

March 22nd

Drank too much coffee today.

Meg came and asked me if sometimes I look at the world and want to understand it better. I said that I did, sometimes, but that it could be hard to find the answers. Her face became bright then, and she said, *Yes, yes, yes, exactly – it is hard to find the answers. But we have to keep looking. That's what we are doing here, you see?* I didn't want to tell her about my parents and I felt a bit shaky, so had to make my excuses then.

Also, noticed that she wears a pass around her neck that lets her through the locked doors. When she has lunch she takes it off and puts it on the table.

March 23rd

Today we talked about particles. I didn't want to mention the micro black holes in case she realised my purpose, but it was okay to talk about the other particles.

She said that when the hadrons collide and smash all sorts of other things will be created. It's like breaking apart a Kinder Egg and finding surprises inside. She told me about some of them, like the Higgs boson (I knew that one) and the quark-gluon plasma and the dark matter. I asked her if she thought it was dangerous to mess with hadrons like this, but she laughed. *Hadrons are everywhere,* she said. *They are not dangerous. They make up you and me. They're just protons and neutrons, they are the building blocks of the world.* That made me a little bit angry, so I sat on my hands. Why then, I thought, why must you break the hadrons apart? It is not good, to break particles apart, to transform them into other things. But before I could say the words she had to go to her lab again to do I-don't-know-what. Maybe she could see that I was angry. Maybe she won't come again.

She reminds me of granny Meg in other ways too, not just that her name is almost the same. Mag. I wrote it wrong before. Her name badge used to say Margarette, she told me, but she prefers Mag because everyone can pronounce that. They have people from all over the world at CERN. But then at lunch I got it wrong anyway, when I said hello, so I explained to her about how Meg was easier for me to remember because of granny Meg, and she said that it was okay for me to call her that.

March 25th
Waited all through lunchtime for two days in the cafeteria but Meg did not come.

March 26th
In the cafeteria today Meg saw me. I thought at first she wasn't going to come over, but then she did. I told her I had been doing lots of reading about hadrons, but that I still thought it was all a bit dangerous. Meg shook her head. She picked up my hand and put it on her arm and said, *You see, my hadrons do not hurt you.* I replied that maybe they would, if they broke apart.

Some of the other scientists came over to our table then, and they were talking to her in French and laughing a lot. She looked sort of sorry for a second and then said something back to them. I don't know what the words were but I think she told them to go away. They waited for her by the door though, and she didn't stay much longer after that.

When she had gone I thought about the little hairs on her arm, and the way they made it hard for me to pull away. Maybe they were statically charged – that happens sometimes, with hairs. I've read that. It would explain the feeling.

March 27th
Finally had the courage to ask her about the black holes. She was at the table with the other scientists but when she saw me waiting for her she came over and I asked her straight away, because for me it was Now or Never.

She smiled when I said about them, like she thought I was a child or something, but I didn't mind too much. She said that they were trying to create new particles that could teach us new things about the universe, but that none of it was dangerous. She said that no black holes would be created, but then she looked thoughtful for a bit and said, *Well, actually, micro black holes might be created, but if they can be created by us then they are everywhere already, all around us, and they are harmless.*

That made me think of black holes everywhere, sucking things away. Maybe that is what happens when people disappear. I said that bad things do happen sometimes, and maybe that is because of the black holes, or maybe it is because of the people and other things that we don't understand.

Well, nothing bad is going to happen here, she said, *but something really good might, because we are going to get some answers.*

I like the sound of that, actually.

I thought for a second that she might touch my hand again, but she didn't − she just smiled at me and I think maybe I smiled back.

March 28th

Granny Meg used to say that questions were good things. Other people would always tell me to stop with all the questions, when I was little, but not granny Meg. I remember that. I think it is maybe why she took me in after mum and dad were gone.

March 29th

Stole Meg's pass today. She was talking to the other scientists and she just left it on the table. I know she won't mind that I took it. And it's not for the reasons you think − I have gone off the word sabotage. Meg understands. She might have even done it deliberately. I believe we have the same purpose, now. I don't want to hurt anyone, I just want to be a part of things and maybe to understand a bit better. I have decided to wear my bow tie to show my good intentions and I have left granny Meg's muffin recipe in my diary in the hotel room, so that it will be passed on.

I'm going to try to sleep now but I don't know if I will be able to. All the energy is making me uneasy, but in a good way. Tomorrow morning, I will stand inside the largest circle on earth and wait for the answers to come.

ART MISTAKES I NEVER LEARN FROM

(NO MATTER HOW OFTEN I MAKE THEM)

KELLIE HUSKISSON

WHEN YOU'VE BEEN MAKING REALLY GOOD PROGESS ON A PIECE... AND THEN YOU GO COLD WHEN YOU REALISE –

...OH NOOOO

YOU FORGOT TO SWITCH LAYERS. ALL YOUR INKS ARE WITH YOUR SKETCHY PENCIL MARKS AND THERE'S NO CHOICE BUT TO START OVER.

FINAL INKS

BLUE PENCIL

I CAN PUT MY DRINK AND MY GROSS INKY/PAINT WATER IN TOTALLY DIFFERENT CUPS, PLACE THEM MILES APART ON MY DESK AND YET, MORE OFTEN THAN NOT...

I END UP WITH A MOUTHFUL OF MURKY PAINT WATER

MOST OF THE TIME, I GET COMPLETELY ABSORBED IN MY WORK WHEN I'M DRAWING. THAT CAN BE A BAD THING WHEN I'M WORKING DIGITALLY...BECAUSE I'M TERRIBLE AT REMEMBERING TO SAVE AS I GO.

AND YOU CAN GUARANTEE, BEFORE I REMEMBER TO SAVE MY WORK, PHOTOSHOP WILL FREEZE UP AND CRASH OR I'LL GET "BLUE SCREEN OF DEATH"-ED BY MY LAPTOP AND THAT'LL BE A GOOD FEW HOURS OF MY LIFE LOST FOR NOTHING!
(ONE OF THE REASONS I PREFER OLD FASHIONED PAPER & INK!)

UUUUGH, HOW DO I NEVER LEARN?!

THE WORST (WELL, BEST) IS THINKING I CAN WORK WITHOUT INTERRUPTION WHEN MY CAT IS AROUND.

IF SHE DECIDES IT'S HER BED THEN I'VE JUST GOT TO WAIT IT OUT. I'M NOT A MONSTER!

GUESS I'M DONE FOR AWHILE, THEN.

YOU AND

YOU AND I

LORI ENGLAND

It starts with the missing words.

There's a word for it, I'm sure, this crumbling of the mind, but my words are in short supply, always tantalisingly at the tip of my tongue, but absent all the same. I can feel the shape of them in my mouth, taste their texture, but translating that into verbal communication is another thing altogether.

I put it down to tiredness at first. Working too hard and letting Luna sleep in my bed even though she can sleep well enough on her own. But it's just the two of us against the world now and I am happier with her tangled in my arms, eyelashes touching her soft cheeks, her quick, quiet breath tickling my ear. If I can feel the whole of her three-year-old self pressed up against me, invading every inch of space, then I know she is safe.

Then I can't remember if I've locked the door or turned off the house controls and not just in the vague, dithery, did-I-or-didn't-I of before, but total, terrifying blackness. Holes where mundanity should be. The thing is, I'm too young for this – this terrifying, slow erosion of memory. Pieces of me are falling out, littering the path behind me.

* * *

It takes you a minute to steel yourself. The kettle whistles quick and harsh, calling time on any pondering. It's such a contrast to all the polished surfaces, this battered stovetop kettle. But that's how he insists tea must be made.

"None of this synthetic shite."

There's no use explaining to him that it's a different delivery system, that the result is the same boiling water meets teabag and then milk is splashed in, but for him there's alchemy in his mother's stovetop kettle. And it's his way or the highway, as he's so fucking fond of saying.

You whisper, "The highway … " as you tip scalding water on your hands and let the kettle fall to the floor. The 'thunk' reverberating pleasantly along the polished echo chamber. You don't scream, just calmly start pouring cold water onto your hands to get the heat out. The crash was enough to call him and you've had enough practice at not crying out.

Sure enough, he saunters in.

"What did you do, woman?"

"Just an accident, burnt my hands a wee bit."

He grabs them out of the cold water and you feel an immediate twinge from the damaged tissue. You're waiting for the numbness to wear off, for every sinew to scream awake.

"C'mon, Cherry, baby. We'll get you to Mason Infirmary. They've got that machine now that fixes burns in a few minutes."

You know where the button is: by the left side of the bed. You memorised it last week at the library. Once you get there, you will press it, just so, and you will be free.

* * *

In a quiet room with lavender light and the aural itch of soothing water sounds playing in the background, I feel around inside my head for the memories that should have been implanted from the bank. The ones on the tick list next to my bed.

Soon enough, my head is swimming with them, old memories slapped down like photographic prints on a table. Except they tell the story of a life I do not recognise.

"They aren't mine," I say. My voice is small, brittle, ready to crack.

"Everyone feels like that at first. You just need to rest and ease into it," says the nurse at my side. Her smile is kind, her words routine and comfortable. I can tell she's said this time and time again and it almost puts my mind at ease. Almost.

I can remember the procedure. I was lucid then, bare legs touching cold sheets as I slid into the machine.

"Quick and painless," the nurse had said, her voice low, soothing. "In just a moment, you'll go to sleep and then for about an hour you'll be connected to the machine, which will slowly feed your previously recorded memories into your consciousness. Afterwards, these will swim to the front of your mind. It will be as though you are living each of those moments again. It can take about a week for the memories to settle, but once they are there, they should stick for good. This is the first procedure of many, so soon you should be an old hand. Okay, Enid, are we good to go?"

I swallow, nod and give a grimace that will have to do for a smile. I know all of this already, of course, but they like to repeat everything in case it's the most recent moment that's blown away like smoke.

* * *

You take her hand. It's late and you've never been more awake. It's come out of nowhere: lights flashing pink to blue, ceiling so close you could taste it and the base buzzing somewhere snugly under your ribcage. And her fingers curled around yours, you aren't sure who's holding who tighter, but you know you are never letting go.

You aren't really sure how you got here, it wasn't planned and it's a million miles from the careful life you've been living. You don't need to hide anymore, but you guard your freedom like a hawk, watching it minute by minute. Each laugh that bubbles up in your chest, you count like the spoils of victory.

But here, right now, there is no place for careful planning and though this feels like it has come out of nowhere, maybe it is a series of small steps, of shared smiles and sideways stares. Two ships grazing past in the glint of daylight, now intertwined safely in the night. Nothing has ever felt quite so important as the texture of her. Beads of sweat roll steadily across your skin and she feels slippery under your fingers, but there's no chance you are letting her go.

* * *

I don't know where you end and I begin.

I mean, I know the facts, some of them anyway. I am Enid, you are not. I am 32 and you are 45. You have three sons and I have Luna. You are Cherry, maybe. At least that's what she calls you in a breathless sigh. It could be a pet name or a shortening. Is it short for anything? I can't remember. I can't remember if I know. I feel like I know you. Of course I do. You're in my head.

And it's not so bad, the ones where I know it's you, the ones where I can distinguish you from me. It's the ones where I don't know which of us the memory belongs to that are the worst. I feel like I'm sliding out sight.

* * *

"Mu-u-u-u-mmy, this dinosaur has no head. Did another dinosaur eat it, Mummy? Rarr!"

"You better check and see if there's a T … T … Oh, god, it's gone … "

"T-Rex. Silly Mummy, losing all the words."

"Silly me. See if there's one in the bottom of the box. Dig deep, pet."

I try not to be embarrassed: it's why I'm here, after all. Luna continues to dig through the box of dilapidated toys that sits in the corner of the doctor's office. I'm not sure how I feel like I've failed her, but I do. This runs in the family, but I should have had another twenty years or more until …

I've been diligent, though, and backed up memories every month down at the warehouse.

"It's rare for it to present so strongly at your age – even among those with such a family history. I'm recommending immediate memory immersion therapy. It's lucky you have stored so many memories. It will be one week on and one week off for several weeks, depending on the results."

"It's not luck." My voice is crisp and untethered from my body. "None of this is luck."

I've started to worry about a different kind of forgetting, the kind my daughter will do each week we are apart.

* * *

"Enid, I'm sorry, but I don't think the procedure has worked as well as we would like," the doctor says, trying for a kindly smile, but it comes off more a smirk. His eyes are made owlish by his oversized glasses.

"'As well as we would like?' I have someone else's memories and I don't seem to have any more of mine. I would say it's an out-and-out failure,' I retort, aiming for reasonable, missing the mark. My fingers knit reflexively into my blue hospital gown. I am underdressed for this party, him in a suit and me in a blue, slithery child's painting apron. I feel like it's to keep me permanently on the back foot.

"We aren't totally sure what has happened, Enid. As you know, the procedure can stir up dormant memories. Ones long buried," he continues, shifting gear into straight out patronising. I hate my name in his mouth. He uses it like a weapon to placate me. He may as well be saying I'm imagining it. At least then, it would be a statement I could challenge.

"Yes, I do know. But that's not what has happened here. It could account for some of it. There are … there are things I'm not sure of. But my head is full of someone else's life, someone else's loves and hates and desires, and I am finding it hard to disentangle them from my own."

I say all this wild-haired, wild-eyed. Shattered, fractured from seven days of someone else's memories crashing round my head.

"I think the best course of action is to begin your second set sooner than expected."

"Is that safe?"

"It's not the usual course we like to follow, but it I think it's wise in this case. It does mean you'll need to stay with us a little longer – another week at least."

He is treading careful lines here, ones I can recognise from years of managing customers' expectations. Never saying the wrong words. The meaning's the same, but just sugar coated for ease of swallowing.

"So, no break? Can my daughter, can she … come and visit before the next round of treatment?"

I feel my voice start to break. Fury always drives me directly to tears and the tears always send the fury inwards with vicious force.

"I'm not sure that's the best course of action. You are very disoriented at the moment, understandably so, and it may be unsettling for her. I think it would be wise to wait it out."

I have to clamp my mouth tight shut to keep myself from telling him what I think of his wisdom, feeling suddenly squashed by the realisation that it will be eight more days. Eight more days until I can curl her up in my lap like a cat, match her breath for breath and feel safe and loved.

***

You are sitting on a windowsill with a small boy curled like a cat in your lap, looking out over a strange city.

"How are the big boys, darling?"

"Asleep, finally. They've been running me ragged."

Her voice on the phone, and your smallest child in your lap, make you feel at home even as your eyes slide over the bright lights of a new place. It had seemed so simple, just to take the littlest and keep the big boys in school when you were on the other side of the world. You'll be fine in a day or so, once you have purpose again and aren't stuck hanging around like wet lettuce. So you hang on to the boy in your arms and the texture of her voice as it zips down the line.

"I miss you, Cherry."

* * *

"The procedure has been successful, then," the owlish doctor smiles at me, and it seems genuine. I figure he must be relieved to get rid of me.

It started much the same: dry mouth, bare legs, cool sheets, silver machine. But when I woke, there were pictures of my life lining the walls of my consciousness.

I swam through old memories like they were happening before my eyes, brand new and in vivid colour. All while sitting in this insipid, lavender coloured room. The ones they implant trigger others, buried deep in my subconscious, to come pouring forth. I know where you end and I begin. Mostly. I pick the pieces of me up from the path and stuff them back in haphazardly.

I find you in the warehouse records, filed under 'Bell, Cherry'. Now that I have your name flickering in pixels across the screen, I know that you exist. It's been a long time since I could trust my mind.

* * *

"Luna, pet, don't stand on the chair – here, do you want to sit on Mummy's knee?"

Cherry's sitting there like something out of a dream. I wonder for the millionth time if Cherry is her real name or just because of the red hair that reaches past her waist. She giggles like she's 22, not in her late 40s. It's odd – I know what that feels like, that laugh. A bubble rising and bursting in your chest.

She doesn't know who I am. Just some stranger trying to get her daughter to sit still for five minutes so she can grab a coffee. I almost want to grab her and shout, "I've got bits of you in my head!" Diluted now more and more by pieces of me, but sometimes I'll start saying, "Do-you-remember-when…" before I remember that that didn't happen to me at all.

She knows about the mistake, that her memories went to someone else. I know that. I fought for that. She got paid compensation, the same as me. They settled before they could be taken to a tribunal, and I was almost disappointed – I wanted to look her in her eyes to see if I could see myself. The bits of me that are her.

I wonder if she ever considers where her memories went, or if she even knows that I felt myself falling away. Turning into someone else, turning into her. What would have happened if they had poured more of her into my head?

I can't help but watching her from the side of my eye, listening to the familiar warm crackle of her voice. I want to look her in the eye, reach out and say something, but something stops me.

I haven't got the words.

LATITUDES

LATITUDES

FLEUR BEAUPERT

Today   we are
hiding
in rain

wet patches
of unease   fully secured
slipping

underneath memory   expertly wired

wind-shivered through

we scurry
to somewhere   that watches

all heading
in different directions

unceasing emergency

writing heroics
as a secret inside   you

concealed
in coffee shops   displaced alarm

splashes conversation
into stunned puddles   replicating
at our feet

THE SCARLET CA

THE SCARLET CAP.

(OR)—IN A CLIMATE OF PARANOID EXCITATION. ...

M. D. BOLSOVER

...

café... space (—a... *concourse?* open.—central. (*exposed?*).—bland, pastel, plastic (tables 'n' chairs (angular)). ...).

strange. ... —t' have people—busied-rushed, and *focussed*—mill-flowing (—a dull *surge*) past (round), as y' try t' sit, quiet, relaxed (*try*) amidst, and eat this... —slightly *damp*,—*compressed* 'n' sad (grey) sandwich (flavourless, in th' main)— (hugely) over-priced, and t' drink this bitter, flat coffee. ...
(a victim, then, (again, no doubt), of th' *captive market* economics o' these places. ...).

... —rush-surging (pulse-es) by,... —through t' th' gates (departures).

—(the departures) *lounge*(loung-*es*). ...

flights.

...

sat.—across, here.—from that drab, commercial (airport. captive) bookshop (over). ...

...

—man.

in a red (—a *scarlet*) cap.
(... —*odd*... —?)

(... perhaps in the wake (so to) of *all* those recent (and not so recent now) *events*... —*attacks*. (Iraq, Belgium, Paris...)... —th' world over... and in this... *ongoing*, ...*pervasive*, and longer... *climate*(-atmosphere) of (—*heightened*) paranoid fear (anxiet). ...).

...

man in the red cap. ...

—large, grey, heavy(-looking) grey parker jacket (coat). (*too* heavy f' th' time-season... —? ... —pockets... —*noticeably*—suspiciously—*stuffed* (—bulge.—full). ...

(young-ish). unshaven (rough-rugged).—*sallow*? baggy (slight), 'n' tattered jeans. ...

... —*hanging around* (so to). ... —loiter(-loitering)-lingers in the broad, open entrance of the book store (in front).
(...

—something in... demeanour (yes)-his *stance* (—his *bearing*). ... —a nerv-self-consc.(aware) discomfort (tense, slight). ... —*awkwardness*. ...).

—doesn't go in. (—?).

—*goes* in.

—looks (browses, inattent) at books.—*distracted* (?—a *show* of browsing—perform)... —not *really* looking (paying attent). ... ... —the *act* (action—pretence) in-of browsing (—the "*browse*" ...)... —an attempt (*failed*-failing)—t' look "*natural*"-casual.
(... —the act, ironic, serves to *betray*, and t' *highlight* his nervs-awkward (self-consc.). ...).

(—what *is* under his coat—grey (tee-) shirt? …

—no obvious objects-lumps ('n'-or bumps)… —only a slight paunch (slight). …).

—*does he* mean ill (intent)—? …
(why pretend-ing t' hang around (nerv-obvious self-consc.)—?).

(*watch.*—with (half-) *genuine* nerv-concern. (nervaccelerat (cool, hollow rush-rise) in the chest(-heart) felt. *buzz*(electric) slight sharpen in muscle-sinews (arms). tense in the head(-mind). …

(—entertain half-fantasy visions (semi-involunt) (*play.*—over 'n' over)… —of explosion (sudden (deafening?) burst-roar—deep-heavy concussion (gravitat).

heat. 'n' flame (—a *wave*)…

—sounding the alarm… —"*DOWN!*" (—see it coming, prompt-ed by astute suspicion—foresight)…

—*get* **blacklace** *down* (—my wife. *my* love. …), 'n' *cover*. …
("*heroics*"…

hmm. …).

…

—emerges. 'n'… *hovers* (again).

…

a woman emerges (young, early thirts, perhaps).—glasses.

—and *joins him*. …

—chat-chatting (—casual).
And *walk away*. …

…

—and *relax*. … (—relaxation-*release* (o' nervs pent). …).

…

strange.

—to become (to… entertain, and to (part-*wilfully*) exaggerate) suspicion (-suspicious). …

—on the evidence of no more than a seeming display of social awkwardness (a—*not really knowing what to do with oneself*. …),… —*waiting for the woman with th' glasses*. …

—of the same sort 'n' variety that I, myself, displayed—mere moments-minutes afore… —*waiting*—for **blacklace**,—and, half-sarcastically, browsing *lip-stick* shades outside the (open. fronted) cosmetics store—stand. … (—did anyone *see me* (in that way)… —*?*).

and that that suspicion (—paranoid-paranoiac *excitation*) should be so easily (-readily) *assuaged* by the presence (appearance-appears) of the young woman (with th' glasses).

…

—all kinds of involunt-(only *semi*-consc., semi-controlled-*mastered*), media (—*news* media), 'n' pop-culture inspired, 'n' (apparently,—at least at first) *uncritical* fears 'n' prejudices (—a heightened state, suspense, of prepared paranoid-paranoiac fear) going on in there. …

…

TRY TURNING IT OFF AND THEN ON AGAIN

TRY TURNING IT OFF AND THEN ON AGAIN

SIMON BROWN

It was the falling bodies that tipped Ron off. He had been strolling down the street when one splattered onto the pavement a few feet ahead of him. He wiped the blood from his face and peered closer. From the clothes, it looked like it was a woman. How strange. He tried – unsuccessfully – to step over her without getting red mush on his suede loafers. Tutting, he pulled a handkerchief from his pocket and began to wipe off the gunk.

"Hey, you down there. Out of the way."

Ron surveyed the street. The only people he could see were dead. Where had that shouting come from?

"I'm serious. Out of the way."

It was a woman fifteen storeys up, perched on the ledge, flailing her arms.

Ron smiled and waved back at her. "Oh, hello up there. Nice day we're having."

"Move. I'm jumping."

"Why ever would you do that?"

The woman laughed. The way it rebounded off the tenement opposite made it sound like she had an audience. "Are you blind? Don't you see the numbers?"

"Numbers? No." He scratched his head. "Sorry."

"Surely you can make out the sun though?"

Ron chuckled. He didn't need to look at the sun. He knew it would be the same as it always was: a white-hot circle creeping through the sky. Still, it wouldn't hurt to humour the gal. But when he looked, instead of the sun there was a giant red X, the tips of which went right into the corners of a surrounding white box. A body smashed into the pavement on the other side of the street.

Ron frowned. "It doesn't usually look like that, does it?"

"Of course not. I've half a mind to jump right now and take you with me."

"You still haven't told me why."

"Don't you see?" The woman was shouting louder than ever. "It's not real. None of it's real."

Ron sighed. He had no time for hippies. Especially not after the episode with Marjorie and that vegetarian piccolo player. As he walked away something squelched onto the pavement behind him.

How could none of it be real? Here he was, here were his hands, here were his (ruined) suede loafers, here were some people pillaging the burnt out remains of a supermarket, here was the breeze that blew the scent of sulphur, here was the sky, here was everything.

Except the sun.

It was only one thing. And, judging by his watch, he was now late. Sun or no sun, there was work to be done.

People galloped past him. Ron couldn't help but chuckle to himself. There would be a rational explanation for all of this and when it was finally revealed (by a scientist whose temperament would be reassuringly dour) everyone would feel incredibly foolish. Everyone except for him and all the other rational thinkers in the world.

When he walked through the door of his workplace, however, instead of finding a shiny lobby filled with shoesqueak and throat clearing all he found was a hollow, blank interior.

Ron tiptoed in. "Hello?"

No one replied. His eyes fell on a small white box in the centre of the room. He slunk closer. On it was a sign that read 404.

So the office was temporarily misplaced. So what? He had plenty of files in his briefcase here; he could work on those until the office was restored, perhaps at that charming café round the corner.

It was only when he re-emerged outside that he noticed the gaping chunks in the skyline. Half of one skyscraper was its usual shiny, glassy self; the other was a blurry shoot of bamboo. That was the trouble with this city: you'd turn your back for one minute and some renegade architect would up and butcher everything.

He carried on down the street, sidestepping the huddled, screaming women, and came upon the stooped, shuffling form of Milton Goodhew doddering towards him.

"Good morning," said Ron, lifting his hat. "Nice day we're having."

Milton's magnified bug eyes blinked through their milk-bottle lenses. "Do I know you?"

Ron felt winded. He pressed his face close to Milton's. He smelled of pipe-smoke and brandy. "It's Ron. Busby. From the office."

"Most amusing. Did Busby put you up to this? Man doesn't have a funny bone in his body."

"Don't be such an ass. You know very well it's me."

Milton smiled politely. "If you say so."

"What do you make of all this then?" said Ron, gesturing at the crowd of people who were running past them.

Milton flapped a hand. "A lot of fuss over nothing. I heard one woman crying about the sun not being there. I mean, really: it's still light isn't it, for goodness sake. Those buildings are still there, even if they do look a little squiffy. It's the signs. They're all jumbled up."

A car came flying down the street, its horn blaring in short, staccato bursts.

"Curious thing," said Ron, scratching the back of his neck. "Our office doesn't appear to be there."

"What do you mean?"

"It's gone. I went through the doors and there was nothing there. Just a sign and some numbers."

Milton stuck a finger in between his lips. "Oh." There were wild-eyed people running past them, all in the same direction. "Perhaps I'm wrong then. Perhaps we ought to be panicking."

There was a roar that seemed to come from the roots of the city. Things smashed, alarms sounded, and more and more flocks started tearing past them.

"I think we ought to start moving," said Milton, tugging Ron's sleeve. "This way," he said, nipping down a narrow sidestreet with surprising speed. The roar faded at once and was replaced with indistinct televisual babble and the sound of a gale-force wind, even though the air was quite still.

"D'you think we might be panicking a tad prematurely?" asked Ron.

Milton, wheezing, shook his head. "Things are perhaps worse than I'd feared."

All around them were clotheslines strung between buildings, suspended from which were a variety of meats and whole animals that oozed onto the ground below. Between the congealing pools of liquid Ron noticed an ominous absence of cement. What lay beneath their feet instead was a grid-like pattern overlaid on a darkness so deep and complete it seemed to hold spiritual significance. The hell of it all was it still felt like cement ought to.

Ron was so busy staring at the ground he walked right into the distance. He staggered backwards, knocking Milton to the ground. Ron approached the distance again, arms outstretched, scrutinising everything that lay in front of him. Though it joined seamlessly with the alley, beyond a certain point everything was indistinct and didn't appear to have any depth at all. He could press a palm up against what was supposed to be a faraway building.

"Like those old cartoons," said Milton, who had had to get to his feet all by himself and was now panting as a result.

"What cartoons?"

"I think it was a bird of some kind. A wolf chases it. Puts a trompe l'oeil in the middle of the road so the bird runs into it. Or so I recall – haven't seen it since Thomasina was small." He prodded the distance with a finger, then shook his head. "This is very rummy."

"You let them watch cartoons? They rot the mind."

"What nonsense. I pity…"

The roar was back. The two turned to face the entrance to the alley and saw swarms of people charging past, clutching bollards, traffic signs and claymores. They spilled into the alley and surged towards them, weapons raised.

Ron dropped his briefcase, picked Milton up by the waist and threw him through an open window before diving in afterwards, deep into a lake.

He fought his way to the surface and hauled himself onto the land. His clothes were bone dry. Milton was nowhere to be seen. But there was the sun! A big bronze button in the sky, wearing whorls of clouds as a garland. One such whorl twisted its way down through the sky into a chimney on a nearby farmhouse.

It looked strangely familiar, the farmhouse, but everything was muddled around. The kennel should've been flush with the wall beneath the kitchen window, the chimney should've been on the roof instead of sticking out of the side and there were never that many doors, were there?

The air was hot, still and filled with the stench of candyfloss. Trees creaked, insects hummed and there was the faint sound of someone sobbing. Ron followed it, tracing it to an open window that almost certainly wasn't where it ought to have been, behind which sat a boy, crying over a shattered porcelain doll whose name, Ron was certain, was Betty.

He stole away from the window, wiping damp peach-smelling patches from under his eyes, and passed the living room, where a woman talked to a man who had his face buried in a newspaper.

"… the harm? He was happy."

The man put down his newspaper. His face was grey, and all of his features were made up of headline text. "People talk, Bunty."

The air felt scorching. Ron had to chew on it to get it to fit in his lungs and it burned him all the way down. He tried some of the doors. Most didn't open. From the one that did there blew a strong, ragged wind. Ron stepped inside, working his way through a narrow corridor until he emerged on a rooftop some-where. Now there was no detail on anything, only outlines of things, each filled in with the number 404 over and over again. The world twisted and swirled in time with Ron's rapid, shallow breaths.

There were other people on this rooftop, people whose grins stretched round the whole of their faces and whose tears fell in a black slick; people who walked hand in hand with one another off the edge of the building.

There was a lone woman peering over the edge at the outline of the street far below.

"Marjorie?"

The woman turned around. She smiled at him for an instant before stepping off the edge.

Ron clamped his hands round his mouth, stifling a scream. But the hands that were round his mouth were not his own; these had thin, delicate fingers with glittering fingernails.

He screamed again. It came out as laughter.

Ron stepped up onto the ledge, staring at all those tiny 404s down below. Just as he'd mustered the courage to jump, a pedestrian below stopped exactly where he was aiming for.

"Hey, you down there. Out of the way."

CONICCAVE

CONCAVE

LUCY GOODWILL

Life is a complex set of curves and she was currently on the trajectory of a downward loop. Her heaviest thought seemed to change almost hourly, with each passing collection of minutes and seconds dragging her ever closer to an x-axis collision. Every time she thought she had pinned it down, she had found the lowest point, another sensation found its way into the mix and pulled her deeper into solitary reflection.

It had been happening for a while, these tortured waves of her existence. From time to time, after a spell of normality, the world would seem to shift around her and she would feel different for a while. It was as though her body stayed still and yet her mind and her sight and everything else moved slightly to the side. On these days (or weeks, or months) she felt unaligned and off centre and she couldn't quite explain it.

No one else seemed to notice, though. It wasn't clear, it seemed, that everything wasn't alright. The world was slightly tilted and physics wasn't on her side but no one commented. No one stopped her. They all looked at her the same and treated her the same and she would find herself overwhelmed by the normality of it all.

How could people be so calm when nothing was quite right?

It was a foolish, sultry husk of a feeling and yet it lingered like the persistent memory of a particularly bad dream. It weighed on her throughout the seconds and the minutes of every hour of every day, until eventually it would become so heavy that it was all she could think about.

It was the worst thing that had ever happened to her and it had happened at least four times.

It was the worst thing that had ever happened to her and nobody seemed to have noticed.

I

RACHEL PLUMMER

The robot likes to wear pearls
and go out to dinner parties.
You see him in a black cocktail dress,
legs up to here, lounging
against the fashionable interiors
of society darling soirées.
The robot watches YouTube videos
on contouring. He's all cheekbones.
You find his witty small talk sparkling.
He pretends to care about Syria
and Brexit. He vapes.
Goes vegan. Knocks back G&Ts.
The robot doesn't do Facebook.
It only makes him compare his circuitry
to other appliances'.
He doesn't need the hassle; the crushing
sense of inadequacy; the 2am sobbing
into a can of WD40.
Sometimes he blogs
about his early life. The inventor.
The inventor's wife. Laments
that it was all a bit lab-coat-chic,
a bit too Asimov – lots of tests, lots of spelling
his own name for visiting school children.
No selfies. Not nearly
enough pearls.

BIOGRAPHIES

CONTRIBUTOR BIOGRAPHIES

Claire Askew is a poet and writer based in Edinburgh. Her debut poetry collection, *This changes things*, was shortlisted for the Edwin Morgan Poetry Award (2014) and the Saltire Society's First Book of the Year Award (2016). Claire is also a novelist, and her debut novel in progress won the 2016 Lucy Cavendish College Fiction Prize. Claire holds a PhD in Creative Writing and Contemporary Women's Poetry and works as a Scottish Book Trust Reading Champion, based at Craigmillar Library. @onenightstanzas

Fleur Beaupert is an Australian poet and writer whose poetry has appeared in spaces such as *Tangent, Cordite, Regime, Bluepepper* and Bimblebox 153 Birds. Her short plays have been performed at a number of Sydney play festivals, and her play *Dead Time*, devised in collaboration with the cast, was staged at 107 Projects in 2015.

M. D. Bolsover is a freelance writer and editor, based in Edinburgh. He has had short pieces of experimental prose out with *FREAK CIRCUS* Magazine (Edinburgh) and *Into the Void* Magazine (Dublin), and forthcoming in an anthology of experimental, 'multimodal' work with Twelve Winters Press (Illinois), and with a project presenting pieces inspired by the work of Scottish-Italian sculptor Eduardo Paolozzi, in Edinburgh.

Simon Brown is originally from the Highlands, now lives in Edinburgh and is working on a novel.

'S e tidsear àrdsgoil a th' ann an **Seonaidh Charity**. Rugadh agus thogadh e ann an Loch a' Bhraoin ach tha e a-nis a' fuireach ann an Dùn Èideann. Bhuainnich e Duais nan Sgrìobhadairean Ùra ann an 2012 agus tha na sgeulachdan goirid aige air nochdadh ann an danamag.org agus *Northwords Now*. Dh'fhoillsich e a' chiad nobhaileag aige, *An Làmh a Bheir* (Sandstone Press 2016) mar phàirt dhen t-sreath *Lasag*.

Seonaidh Charity is a secondary school teacher who lives in Edinburgh but was born and brought up in Lochbroom. He was awarded 'Duais nan Sgrìobhadairean Ura' in 2012 and his short stories have appeared in danamag.org and Northwords Now. His first novella, *An Làmh a Bheir*, was published by Sandstone Press in 2016 as part of the *Lasag* series.

Beth Cochrane is an Edinburgh based fiction writer. She graduated, with Distinction, from the MSc Creative Writing programme at the University of Edinburgh in 2015. She is the winner of the Sloan Prize 2015 and is one of Edinburgh City of Literature's Story Shop writers, 2016. She performed her work at the Edinburgh International Book Festival this summer. @literature_wine

C. Scott Davis is a writer, computer programmer, game designer, humorist (of dubious quality), composer/musician (even more dubious), and generally interested in almost everything. He has successfully completed NaNoWriMo six times, and has attempted (and failed) the July version twice.

Glasgow-based writer **Karyn Dougan** was 2016's New Writers Callan Gordon Award Winner. She has written for The List, The Skinny and The Bear, and has worked in almost every section of the book industry as a proofreader, editor, reviewer and bookseller. Her first short story was published in *Alight Here: An Anthology of Falkirk Writing* (Cargo, 2015).

Lori England is a writer and poet from Glasgow, Scotland. Her work has been published in Pankhearst's Fresh column, by *Crab Fat Magazine* and was shortlisted for the 2015 Bold Types creative writing competition. She is currently juggling studying English Literature and Creative Writing at the Open University with bringing up her own tiny girl gang. Find her work at lori-england.tumblr.com

Ali George is a writer and sometime comicker from Edinburgh. In 2015 she read at the Edinburgh International Book Festival as part of the Story Shop programme of emerging writers. You can find her work in *Freak Circus*, *Lies Dreaming*, *Dactyl*, and all over the internet. She tweets @12books12months and blogs at 12books12months.com

Elizabeth Gibson is a Masters student at the University of Manchester and a Digital Reporter for Manchester Literature Festival. She is a member of Writing Squad 8 and her work has appeared in *The Cadaverine*, *London Journal of Fiction*, *NowThen*, *Far Off Places*, *Myths of the Near Future*, *The Mancunion*, *Octavius*, *Severine*, *Halo* and *Ink, Sweat and Tears*. @Grizonne

Lucy Goodwill is a writer and charity worker, based in North East London. An avid reader and literature graduate, her work primarily consists of poetry and flash fiction. @lucygoodwill

Thomas Heitler is from Newport-on-Tay, Scotland. He graduated with a degree in Painting from Robert Gordon University, and he now spends most of his time drawing cartoons, drinking large amounts of coffee, and updating his portfolio on thomasheitler.carbonmade.com

Kellie Huskisson is a Birmingham based artist and comic creator who's really into space, witches, and cats. She currently enjoys making comics about all of those things and more! She also has an on going series of books illustrating inspirational women who light up her life. @k_doodles_art

Gavin Inglis writes mostly for interactive media, working on smartphone fitness game Zombies, Run! and Victorian tea-break epic Fallen London. His punchy fiction collection of ineffective apparitions, *Crap Ghosts* is available in paperback or ebook. Gavin's recent work includes a novel-length teen revenge story, *Neighbourhood Necromancer*, and a New Media Scotland funded mental health piece, *Hana Feels*. www.gavininglis.com @gavininglis

Deena E. Jacobs is a Canadian artist who spends her time drawing and painting while listening to her record collection and eating delicious food. Having previously resided in Japan (2009-2010), Scotland (2010-2013) and Spain (2014-2016), she has recently returned to Canada where she continues to explore and enjoy the everyday.

Jonathan Macho is an English Graduate who lives in Cardiff with his family and a burgeoning civilisation of books. He has previously been published in the *To Hull and Back* 2016 anthology, the *Beneath the Surface* short story collection by Candy Jar Books, and Pageturners India's *Across the Ages*.

Ian McKenzie lives in the East Midlands after being born and raised in Perth. He has written poetry for the podcast, Lies, Dreaming, *Raum Magazine*, and the *In Praise of Nedd Ludd* anthology amongst others. He has also exhibited mixed-media sculptures for Glasgow's Toaty Wee Exhibition and *FTP Magazine*.

Tha **Robbie MacLeòid** na òranaiche agus sgrìobhadair, a tha a' rannsachadh aig Oilthigh Ghlaschu. Tha e air duaisean a chosnadh airson a chuid òrain, leithid co-fharpaisean sgrìobhadh a' Mhòid, agus co-fharpais Hands Up For

Trad, 'Nòs Ùr'. 'S ann às a' Ghàidhealtachd a tha e, agus tha e an-diugh a' fuireachd air a' Ghalldachd.

Robbie Andrew MacLeod is a songwriter and writer, studying at the University of Glasgow. He has won prizes for his songs, including competitions at the Mòd, and Hands Up For Trad's 'Nòs Ùr' competition. He is from the Highlands, and lives in the Lowlands.

Kevin MacNeil is an award-winning writer, originally from the Outer Hebrides. His work includes novels, poetry, aphorisms, plays, songs and screenplays. His latest novel is *The Brilliant & Forever*. KevinMacNeil.com @Kevin_MacNeil

Jen McGregor is a playwright and director whose recent credits include *Vox* (Charioteer Theatre/Piccolo Theatre of Milan) and *Heaven Burns* (Previously… Scotland' History Festival). Her short play *Love Love*, the story of a dangerously lovelorn SatNav, was published in *New Writing Scotland #34* in August 2016.

Cara L McKee was born in Yorkshire, and now lives in Largs, Ayrshire, with her young family. She writes a column for *Scotland 4 Kids* magazine and on ohwedo.blogspot.co.uk. She has been published in *The Fat Damsel*, won a Writing Umbrella poetry competition and is now writing her first novel. @caramckee

Chris McQueer is a sales assistant and writer from Glasgow. Some of his work is forthcoming in *The High Flight* literary fanzine and in *The Football Pink* magazine. When he isn't selling shoes, busting queues or writing weird short stories for strangers on the internet, you can most likely find him spouting nonsense at parties with a bottle of Buckfast in hand. You can read more of his short stories at medium.com/@ChrisMcQueer

Christina Neuwirth was born in Austria and now lives in Edinburgh. After completing an MSc in Creative Writing in 2014, she started working at Scottish PEN and at the University of Edinburgh. Her work has been published in *Gutter* and on Commonspace.scot, and her novella *Amphibian* is currently shortlisted for the LJMU/MMUC Novella Award. In her spare time, she enjoys roller skating, baking and hanging out with cats.
 www.christinaneuwirth.com @gwynn255

Jamie Norman is an Edinburgh-based poet. His work has appeared in *Gutter*, *Causeway/Cabhsair*, *Abridged* and others. He loves all things Vintage and tweets from @normantweets

Nicholas J. Parr is a former architecture student that recently rediscovered a lost passion from his youth; reading and writing stories. You can see more of his work at nicholasjparr.com

picklish is a scientist – one who hopes to bring things into existence by writing about them first. He doesn't mind who makes real the contents of his fiction, but hopes that by writing he will encourage himself and others to make the physical world a little more … odd.

Rachel Plummer has had poems published in magazines including *Mslexia*, *The Stinging Fly*, *Agenda*, *Dactyl* and *RAUM*. She is a Troubadour prizewinner, twice runner up in the Penfro Poetry Competition and placed third for the Canterbury Festival Poet of the Year. She is a recipient of the Scottish Book Trust New Writers Award for poetry. She has received a cultural commission from LGBT Youth Scotland. www.rachelplummer.co.uk @smaychel

Max Scratchmann is a British writer and illustrator. His poems and short stories have appeared in many anthologies and literary magazines, including the Edinburgh literary quarterly, Chapman and Iron Press' anthology, *Star Trek – The Poems*. He co-runs the performance poetry company, FREAK Circus; and his poem 'Snow Globes' was included in the Dear Scotland International writing awards.

Helen Sedgwick is the author of *The Comet Seekers* and has an MLitt in Creative Writing from Glasgow University. She won a Scottish Book Trust New Writers Award in 2012, and her writing has been broadcast on BBC Radio 4 and widely published in magazines and anthologies. helensedgwick.com @helensedgwick

Katerina Sidorova is a visual artist, currently based in the Netherlands, and a recent graduate of the Royal Academy of Art in The Hague. More information and work can be found on katerina-sidorova.com

Alice Tarbuck is a writer living in Edinburgh. Most recently, she has been shortlisted for the Jupiter Artland Poetry Prize, and work is forthcoming from *Zarf*, *3elements Review* and *The Plum Tree Tavern*. @atarbuck

THANK YOU

THANK YOU TO OUR PATRONS

These fine folk not only supported 404 Ink before there was even a mention of a magazine, they also put their money where our big mouth is. By pledging an amount per issue, they helped us get the 404 ship sailing, print a lot of lovely artists in a magazine and pay them all for the pleasure of sharing their work with you all, and for that we are eternally grateful. Give a big round of applause to:

Claire Askew
Nicola Balkind
Nicole Brandon
Catriona Cox
Liam Alastair Crouse
Muireann Crowley
Morven Gow
Rosie Howie
Michaela Hunter
Inside The Bell Jar
Peter Kerr
Kirstin Lamb
Jennie May
Mairi McKay
Kerry McShane
Jamie Norman
Daiden O'Regan
Almond Press
Victoria Sinden
Kirstyn Smith
Claire Squires
Elizabeth Stanley
Emma Swann
Mark Wrightman

And a number of patrons who choose to remain anonymous.

SUBSCRIBE TO 404 INK

As mentioned in the opening editorial, we currently use the crowdfunding platform Patreon as a means of offering a subscription service to the twice-yearly magazine. If you enjoyed this first issue of *404 Ink*, would like to be signed up for the next, and receive all the gossip and info about upcoming publications first, then Patreon is the place to be!

How does Patreon work?
So glad you asked. On Patreon you pledge to give a creator a chosen amount of money either per month or per creation. We currently have our Patreon set up so we receive all pledges when the magazine issue is complete and ready to be sent out to readers. This is twice a year, in November and May.

You can pledge $1 to receive all the behind-the-scenes updates before anyone else, $5 for the ebook, $10 for the printed magazine (UK only) or $20 for the printed magazine if you're outside of the UK. (Patreon is a US company so pledges are in dollars, but they convert the currency, and it works wherever you are in the world!). All patrons are the first to hear about any news or reveals we may have.

When we're ready to send the magazine to subscribers we press the big red button which will send all pledged money to us – unlike normal subscriptions, we don't see any money until the magazine's ready, so you're not paying for anything until we have it ready for you in all its glory.

So why Patreon?
We're using Patreon because it's a public platform that brings transparency and accountability to the creative process. It means we have a direct relationship with our readers, we know that there's money coming in to help us pay our authors and it spreads the word about all those talented folks. We hope you'll hop on board.

www.patreon.com/404ink

THE F WORD

The fun doesn't end here. Submissions are open for Issue 2 of *404 Ink*, coming in May 2017. The theme is The F Word. What that word might be is up to you.

Fame.
Feminism.
Fucking.
Fancy.
Friends.
Failure.
Flip.
Fantastical.
Fork.
France.
Frippery.
Fret.
Forlorn.
Frank.
Farewell.
Facebook.
Feck.
Fluff.
Fall.
Foreign.
Falafel.
Forever.

If you're a writer or artist and would like to submit for Issue 2, please do! We're accepting short stories, poetry, narrative non-fiction and comics in English and Scottish Gaelic. If you'd like to be published in a magazine very much like this one, we are awaiting your email. For more details on submissions guidelines and deadlines, visit 404ink.com/submissions